THE JERUSALEM STONE
OF CONSCIOUSNESS

DMT,
Kabbalah &
the Pineal Gland

JOEL DAVID BAKST

City of Luz Publications www.cityofluz.com

ISBN-13: 978-1489543776
ISBN-10: 1489543775

All images and graphics were either created by the author or taken
from the public domain and altered or taken from the public domain and unaltered. If any image should be credited, please inform us and we will be happy to do so in future editions.

(The current edition was previously published as
*The Foundation of Jewish Consciousness:
Kabbalah, the Pineal Gland & Jerusalem of the Mind*)

Dedication

Following the providential confluence in the summer of 1967 of The Six Day War and the "Summer of Love", thousands of young Jews were reawakened to a lost heritage. They were the first wave of the *Ba'al Teshuvah* movement who had returned to the Land and Torah of Israel. Some came in search of or stumbled upon an ancient tradition of the *Ohr HaGanuz* — the hidden light of rapturous Jewish God-consciousness. Although rediscovering their Judaism, a new life and spiritual contentment, along the way most ceased believing that they could ever directly experience that Divine Light.

This book is dedicated to those who never abandoned the search for directly experiencing the ecstatic light at the end of the Torah tunnel.

Contents

Disclaimer

DMT (dimethyltryptamine) is a neurotransmitter produced naturally within every human body. Possession of synthetically produced DMT, as well as DMT derived from certain plants, is currently illegal and its usage violates the law in the U.S.A. and in most countries around the world. Any reference in this book to DMT is referring to DMT originating from within the human body and nowhere advocates the usage of externally produced DMT. Moreover, references to human DMT are intended only as an analogical model to understand how to practice a meditative technique that is part of the ancient Jewish esoteric tradition. Also note that the relationship of DMT to the pineal gland is a contemporary medical hypothesis that, although there is strong supporting evidence, has yet to be scientifically proven.

Preface

The Jerusalem Stone of Consciousness — DMT, Kabbalah and the Pineal Gland welcomes the reader to embark upon a pilgrimage to the holiest site in the world — Jerusalem. The Jerusalem I am referring to is not first and foremost the 3,000 year old geographical city of Jerusalem, the capital of ancient and modern Israel. Rather, this pilgrimage is to another Jerusalem — the Jerusalem of the Mind — the holiest site in the *inner* world of every man, woman, and child. However, the Jerusalem of the Mind is a secret passageway — a cosmic wormhole — that leads directly to the global Jerusalem, and then, like the infinity sign, loops back again to every individual's Jerusalem of the Mind.

Unexpectedly, this pilgrimage begins within the smallest and most mysterious organ in the human body — the pineal gland sequestered away in the middle of the cranium. The pilgrimage ends with a small but the most controversial piece of property on the planet — the Foundation Stone that is sequestered away in the middle of a large, cranium-like dome in the middle of Jerusalem.

Although various parts of the human body produce the unique substance called DMT (dimethyltryptamine), current research suggests that the major source for DMT is the pineal gland. The Foundation Stone, according to ancient Biblical prophesies, is destined to deliver a unique substance called *Mayim Chayim*— "Living Liquid". The Foundation Stone, also known as *Peniel*— literally, the Face of God — loops back into its beginning and returns us to the foundation of our own consciousness. This is the P2P Principle — Pineal to Peniel and back again.

The Jerusalem Stone of Consciousness is, in many ways, the culmination of my forty year search for a light at the end of a very long tunnel. As a teenager I explored both Oriental and Occidental esoteric doctrines and practices. I researched non-ordinary states of consciousness experiencing momentary visions of transcendence. I caught glimpses of, for lack of a better expression, an other-dimensional light of pure, ecstatic, God-consciousness. Yet, aside from those brief revelatory periods, that other-world luminosity was light-years away from the shards and shells of my everyday existence.

Decades later the light of consciousness that I had experienced as a younger man was rediscovered through the technology of Jerusalem of the Mind. In retrospect, I realized that the source of those episodes of higher consciousness were sparks of the actual *Ohr HaGanuz* — the redemptive Hidden Light — the messianic light of higher-dimensional consciousness.

Following my initial encounters I began a pilgrimage in search of that universal light of consciousness. Unexpectedly my path took me to the geographical Jerusalem where I ended up living and studying for two decades. It was in the *yeshivot* (seminaries) and study halls of the holy city that I was introduced to a treasure house of ancient exoteric and esoteric "maps" — Torah, Talmud, and Kabbalah. Endless worlds within eternal words opened before me as I was initiated into the nearly 4,000 year old tradition.

Yet, even though I was living in the center of Jerusalem — the millennial crossroads of consciousness, cultures, and conflicts there remained another center, another crossroads that was somehow missing. Through decades of Talmud and Kabbalah study I learned how to access and master multitudes of maps that probed virtually every aspect of creation. However, as mind-boggling and life-changing as this knowledge and initiation was, and as much as it had transformed my life (and many others' lives), I could barely see the territory for the map.

My pilgrimage to the spiritual center of Jerusalem and into the veiled worlds of the Talmudic Sage-Mystics was incomplete.

It remained so until I began to put together hundreds, if not thousands, of seemingly unrelated kabbalistic components and rabbinic formulas that I had amassed over decades long study and exploration into prayer and meditation. It was only then with great passion, persistence, and prayer, that I rediscovered another Jerusalem — the spiritual twin, the soul to the physical Jerusalem — Jerusalem of the Mind.

After forty years of searching, the P2P principle has been for me the only complete multi-dimensional system of higher Torah-based consciousness that meets all the extremely demanding and highly critical inter-disciplinary criteria. P2P is a spiritual technology that is rigorous in its logic, scientific in its approach and unexpectedly powerful in its effects. Jerusalem of the Mind is at the same time both ancient and futuristic. It has taken forty years to find the light at the end of the tunnel, but thank God, it has occurred in this lifetime. An equal, if not greater, source of gratitude is that I am able to share Jerusalem of the Mind with others who also desire to enter into this sacred work and make a pilgrimage along the royal road to the New Jerusalem of the Mind.

x

Introduction

The Jerusalem Stone of Jewish Consciousness introduces a methodology — an inner technology — that produces a distinct state of consciousness. This system is Jerusalem of the Mind — JeM for short. The operating mechanism is referred to as the P2P principle — Pineal (gland) to Peniel (the Foundation Stone).

P2P is a unique form of meditation, yet it is more than meditation.

It is a powerful mode of prayer — easily integrated into traditional daily Hebrew *tefilah/davenin* — yet it is more than prayer.

It is a vehicle for inter-dimensional travel, yet the participant does not physically go anywhere.P2P

It is based upon a secret kabbalistic doctrine, yet it is solidly anchored in traditional Judaism.

It is capable of generating a profound ecstatic experience, yet no external drugs are necessary.

It mitigates anxiety and depression, yet it is much more than self-help therapy.

It takes you to the center of your true self, yet it simultaneously centers you within the whole of all humanity.

It is an all-encompassing model of Torah-based Jewish consciousness, yet it is expansively universalistic.

It is for Jews, yet it is also for non-Jews.

It produces a non-ordinary state of higher consciousness, yet it can be used even while engaged in the most mundane activities.

The P2P principle is as mystical as it is scientific and it as ancient as it is futuristic. It unites modern Western discovery with ancient Eastern wisdom. JeM is purifying, redemptive, and truly messianic.

This book maps a clear and detailed system that can provide access to a non-ordinary transcendent state of being. This state can produce bliss, inner visions, encounters with benevolent entities, and endless cascading levels of God-consciousness. Entering into Jerusalem of the Mind, however, is not just for one's own well-being, pleasure, and enlightenment (and to maintain sanity in an ever chaotic and ominous world). The sacred work of P2P is also a momentous responsibility. This work is true *tikun olam* — rectification of one's personal world within, and rectification of, our global world without. Each one of us is in a daily battle for individual consciousness and all of us are in a daily battle for global consciousness. Jerusalem of the Mind is also a call to inner arms.

From a traditional Torah perspective this book offers nothing new. To the contrary, the strength of this system and practice is that it is simply an updated application of an ancient, unbroken transmission. *The Jerusalem Stone of Consciousness* does nothing more than assemble an array of Talmudic and Kabbalistic formulas. I have utilized the rigorous rabbinic methodology in which I was trained together with advanced teachings from Kabbalah masters that I have received. I have been able to achieve this otherwise impossible task only by scrutinizing their statements and formulas through the templates of the cutting-edge New Sciences. The synergistic unification of these three disciplines Talmud, Kabbalah, and the New Sciences — has enabled me to decipher a long series of codes that the Sage-Mystics of the Talmud, Midrash, and Zohar have ingeniously encoded into their recorded discussions.[1]

In every generation, there has been an elite cadre of Kabbalah and Talmudic masters who were initiates of these secret traditions. Yet, for the most part the "masters of concealment" hermetically sealed "mounds upon mounds" of critical esoteric data throughout the width and breadth of their vast tomes. Much of this data has been lying dormant since the two Talmuds were closed (the 4th and 5th centuries C.E.) anxiously waiting the moment to become manifest.

This "data encoding", often in the guise of outwardly preposterous stories and bizarre exegesis of scriptural verses, served to keep these doctrines hidden yet transmitted like a time-capsule for a much later generation. That generation, it was understood, would not only vitally need those codes, but it would also have available the tools to comprehend and utilize those codes. That future is now and that generation is us.

The tools — the new maps, models and metaphors, as explained in this book — are being provided to us by the ever-expanding fields of the New Sciences. The P2P formula — Pineal gland to Peniel consciousness and back — is a prophecy fulfilled in our generation. This phenomenon should not surprise us as it is our tradition that, "They [the Talmudic Sage-Mystics] left room for later generations to make their own contributions".[2]

One of the reasons that prompted me to make public JeM and the P2P model is a documentary film in which I appeared. Several years back I was interviewed for *The Spirit Molecule* which has been well-received internationally. (It is accessible via YouTube.com and other venues). The video was inspired by Dr. Rick Strassman's groundbreaking and bestselling book *DMT — The Spirit Molecule*. Strassman's work, together with that of other researchers (e.g., in the fields of ethnopharmacology, neurology, psychiatry, chemistry, anthropology), appears to be an unprecedented discovery in the brain/mind/consciousness sciences.

I was the only interviewee representing a Jewish perspective (as well as the only "theologian" representing any religion). I was asked, from a Jewish and Kabbalah perspective, what is DMT? In my half dozen appearances in the documentary I suggested that the model and the spiritual analog of the DMT phenomenon — not the substance per se — is of profound significance and that it even has a messianic role to play in our generation. Judging from the emails I have received this idea has generated vigorous responses from around the world.

The effects of DMT, whether manufactured externally by plants, or by chemists, or produced endogenously in the human body, are quite profound and literally "out of this world". The experiences that are methodically and scientifically recorded in the book, in the documentary and elsewhere, are so inexplicable that there are virtually no coherent models with which to contextualize them.

The professionally-assessed DMT evidence indicates the following, rather stunning, consensual truths:

- Unlike LSD and most psychoactive substances, the DMT beings, dimensions, and consciousnesses that humans experience are not hallucinations or mental projections.

- Right here and right now, there exists a free-standing, intersecting parallel reality that contains consciousnesses vastly transcending our own.

If the above is indeed the case, then the ramifications are staggering almost beyond comprehension. We don't need to look any further for "close encounters" with something "out there". What we are seeking (or at least the one-in-a-thousand among us) is here within.

Questions, including those that I am repeatedly asked by Jews and non-Jews, are:

- "What am I now supposed to do with this information or with this experience"?

- "What does the Torah — that, as a rule has an answer for everything — have to say about DMT?"

- "Why are we born with DMT in our bodies and what can it reveal to us about our reality and our purpose in life?"

- "What does DMT bode for humanity's immediate future"?

- "Can DMT, with its hypostasized origin in the pineal gland, and its ramifications affect the most intractable, time immemorial, cosmo-geopolitical drama in the Middle East?"

For the tens of thousands around the world who, in one form or another, have experienced this phenomenon the perplexing question is:

"Where do we go from here"?

Reframed more specifically:

"Where does the reality of DMT *take us* from here?"

So, what *is* the next stage for all the deep and disturbing questions that DMT rips open? These questions demand answers, especially from the perspective of the Talmudic Sage-Mystics. An endless array of books, websites, publications, videos, and discussions concerning the mystery of DMT is now available to non-scholars. The common denominator of all this array is that there *is none* — no common denominator, no coherent explanation exist as to what the higher-dimensional roots of DMT are!

The Jerusalem Stone of Consciousness suggests a definitive answer. This book is a detailed study and exploration of what I could only barely touch upon in the documentary. Moreover, the contents of these pages suggest an entire methodology, replete with diagrams and maps, to a long-lost territory. In effect, JeM is an instruction book of how to stimulate endogenous DMT within one's own brain and body.

Most importantly, however, JeM reveals how to stimulate the *spiritual root* of the molecular and material-based DMT. This is the divine substance I call M-DMT — *Messianic* DMT (The letter M also representing *Mosaic* [Moses] and *Metatronic* [Metatron] as elaborated elsewhere in my writings). In these pages, M-DMT is elucidated as the renewed "Living Liquid" (*Mayim Chayim*) foretold by the Hebrew prophets from ancient times. If there was a Jewish equivalent of a Holy Grail, a Fountain of Life, an Elixir of Eternal Youth, or the Divine Light at the end of the cosmic tunnel, Jerusalem of the Mind would be it. In fact, as will be shown, within the soul of the mysterious little pineal organ there lies the hidden portal to *Derech Aitz Chayim* — the path leading back to the original higher-dimensional Tree of Life at the very center of the Garden of Eden.[3] This book is not simply an exciting intellectual excursion. The reader should not mistake the outer map for the inner territory. Rather, *The Jerusalem Stone of Consciousness* is a guidebook to direct experience and direct knowing. These chapters contain parts to be assembled. It is up to the serious pilgrim to follow the instructions, put the chapters and pieces together, plug it in, turn it on, and take off on a deep journey to the secret of one's own inner Jerusalem.

Part I of *The Jerusalem Stone of Consciousness* contains much mapping with some territory; Part 2 details more maps but mostly territory. Important keys are also secreted within the endnotes that must be studied along with the main text.

As the formulas, techniques and inner visionary maps of Jerusalem of the Mind continue to mature, the territory continues to unfold. Even as I write this introduction, additional chapters are being prepared for the next edition. Every individual can build his or her own inner temple of Jerusalem and together help build the collective global higher-dimensional metropolis of the future — the New Jerusalem.

This treasure map, and certainly the treasure itself, does not belong to any one person. The material is "open source" and everyone who enters into this living legacy of the Torah and her Sages can question, challenge, offer new insights, and add additional techniques.

As this practice continues to grow and achieve greater force and coherency, the only prerequisites are a sincere devotion to higher truth, a proper reverence of the Torah, and the application of the methodology and mission of the Jewish Rabbis of the Kabbalah. There truly is a light at the end of a now, not so long, tunnel. That light is a luminous gem for those who can begin to see its universal messianic brilliance and the power of its Godly radiance. It is the JeM of the world. It is Jerusalem of the Mind and the Foundation of Jewish — and World — Consciousness.

Endnotes

1   This unique synergistic union between Kabbalah, Talmud, the New Sciences and their application are explained at length in my book *Beyond Kabbalah – The Teachings That Cannot Be Taught* as well as in my two volume work *The Secret Doctrine of the Gaon of Vilna*.

2   Babylonian Talmud *Chullin* 7a. This phenomenon, of the paradoxical nature
of our generation, is explained in *Beyond Kabbalah – The Teachings That Cannot Be Taught* as well as in *The Secret Doctrine of the Gaon of Vilna*, Volume II.

3   Genesis 3:24

4   Individual and group practitioners of Jerusalem of the Mind are, much in a grass-roots manner, growing and spreading around the world. If you wish to join in the P2P network, the invitation is open.

Jerusalem

PART I
The Foundation Stone

There is information coming forth from the cutting edge of the brain and mind sciences about a mysterious little organ in the middle of the brain known as the pineal gland and an enigmatic substance produced within every human body called DMT. The light these two phenomena shed upon Judaism's most ancient kabbalistic secret — the Foundation Stone in Jerusalem — is truly revelatory and profoundly timely.

1. The Riddle of the New Jerusalem

Our exploration into the pineal gland, the Foundation Stone & Jerusalem of the Mind begins — in a classic Jewish manner — with a question. Even better, it is a type of Talmudic mind puzzle — the Riddle of the New Jerusalem. The one who resolves this challenging kabbalistic quandary is virtually assured an entry into a non-ordinary state of consciousness — a direct experience that leads into the secret inner temple of Jerusalem of the Mind.

> *"The Holy One vowed that He will not enter the
> Celestial Jerusalem until He enters the earthly Jerusalem".*
>
> Talmud[1]

This ancient statement of the Talmudic Sage-Mystics[2] is well known, as is the rabbinic discussion surrounding it that continues until this day. That there exists literally two Jerusalems — a physical one below and a metaphysical or higher-dimensional one above — is also well known throughout the corpus of the Written and Oral Torah. At the center of both Jerusalems is the *Beit HaMikdash* — the Temple. In the language of those initiated into the ancient Talmudic tradition this statement is a formula indicating that there exists an interdependent relationship between the lower and higher dimensional Jerusalem, the latter being the living soul for the former.

This phenomenon is a spiritual mechanism "hardwired" into creation and into the complex and puzzling process of redemption. In today's religious and political climate, however, the mere mention of a future temple in Jerusalem immediately draws battle lines, not just between secular and religious Jews but also within the various observant Torah and Kabbalah circles. One fact is inescapable. Six full chapters of the Book of Ezekiel detail the architectural blueprints for a massive structure in a future New Jerusalem. Additionally, there are many other sources that explicitly or implicitly describe such a structure. Whether or not this compound, known as the Third Temple, will be built from the "ground up" through human effort or from "Heaven down" through Divine will is at the root of the controversy.

The great Jewish legal authority and philosopher Maimonides (13th century), in accord with his rationalistic approach, maintains that human hands will construct the Third Temple.[3] The Talmudic statement quoted above appears to support Maimonides. Maimonides' contemporary the outstanding Biblical commentator Rashi, however, writes that "The Third Temple will be made of [higher dimensional] fire and miraculously descend already built from Heaven".[4] This position, however, is complicated by the fact that there are a number of other authoritative sources that indicate that a third temple will indeed, as maintained by Maimonides, be built by human hands.

Over the last few decades and particularly in the last few years, individuals and groups have invested much time, money and energy toward the goal of actually rebuilding a Third Temple in our lifetime. This movement believes that the Temple must be built from the "ground up". Toward this end, there are those who zealously study the volumes of laws connected with the Temple service and the role the Kohanim (Aaronic priests) and Levites will have in it. The actual vessels and artifacts (e.g., the Ark of the Covenant, the breastplate of the High Priest, the seven-branched candelabra, etc.) have been meticulously constructed according to biblical and legal details. Moreover, a recent poll has shown that even among the Israeli populous (traditional as well as secular), half the people would like the Holy Temple to be rebuilt.[5] Realistically, however, according to the current state of affairs this is virtually impossible. Given the current geopolitical climate, the onset of construction of a third temple, and even discussion of the subject, is not likely to go over quietly in the Islamic world, which currently has, for all practical purposes, total control over the Temple Mount.[6]

In contradistinction to the view that a Third Temple will be built by human effort, there are those sages and schools of Torah thought who rely on the traditions that, "the Third Temple will be made out of "fire" and descend miraculously from Heaven". Moreover, they maintain that it is forbidden to attempt to build it from human hands.[7] However, concerning apparent contradictory traditions of the Talmudic Sage-Mystics it is well known that, "These and those are [both] the words of the Living God". Both rabbinical views are, in fact, simultaneously correct. Both are intentionally recorded, each "opinion" simply viewing one angle or aspect of that which cannot be stated in a single, linear statement. However, if this is true, how can a future temple, "A house for all Nations" be both "natural" and "supernatural" at the same time? How can the Third Temple be built both by man and by God — at the same time? Is our only option to understand the intentionally puzzling and contradictory message of the "masters of concealment" as a "this" or a "that"?

It is proclaimed of the Holy One that, "He's got the whole world in His hands". In this case, His "right hand" embraces the soul of the heavenly temple and His "left hand" holds the body of the earthly temple. Can there be a hidden, secreted "middle hand" of God? Until now, a true synthesis, a "new middle" simultaneously incorporating human consciousness and Divine Will has been virtually inconceivable. Consequentially, often the "wheat has been thrown out with the chaff", i.e., the ancient tradition of a higher-dimensional New Jerusalem has been relegated to the Jewish dustbin of fanciful legends and religious dogma. Even for observant Torah- based Jews, although they may emphatically believe in all the words of the sages, often they have no coherent and "scientific" manner of grasping these "legendary" traditions. However, the confluence between recent scientific and medical discovery from "below" with ancient Torah and kabbalistic truth from "above" reveal a wholly unexpected path. This "path lost for years" may also be the most important secret to Israel's defense and survival. Additionally, this "secret weapon" contains the key to our own enlightenment and higher consciousness. Accordingly, the Talmudic formula that "The Holy One vowed that He will not enter the celestial Jerusalem until He enters the earthly Jerusalem" is an esoteric riddle that only in our generation can be unraveled. Most significantly the secret to this spiritual puzzle can actually be applied right now and directly experienced. This path leads us directly to the threshold of the New Jerusalem

2. The Prophetic Confluence between Kabbalah and Science

The past several decades have brought a great interest in expanded human potential replete with a growing library in what has been called the confluence of mysticism and the "New Sciences". Kabbalah, the Jewish esoteric tradition, has long envisioned and even required an evolving interface between scientific discovery and esoteric truth.

Within the ancient volumes of the Holy Zohar (Book of Radiance, 2nd/13th century) a vision of a new global paradigm is recorded, not to begin unfolding until many centuries in the future:

> In the 6th century of the 6th millennium (i.e., in the years 5,500-5,600 in the Hebrew calendar corresponding to the years 1740-1840 CE.) the gates of wisdom from above (Kabbalah) and the fountains of wisdom from be- low (science and technology) will be opened up and the world will make preparations to enter the 7th millennium just as one makes preparations on the 6th day of the week when the sun is about to set [for the 7th day — the Shabbat].

This passage has been explained by the Talmudic Sage-Mystics of Israel, including the Hassidic masters, as referring to the fact that from the 18th and especially from the 19th century onward the Kabbalah would experience a profound renewal clarifying and rendering more accessible her own esoteric traditions.[8] Any student of contemporary mysticism cannot but be astounded by the recent dramatic accessibility of the Kabbalah and its new and ever increasing popularity.[9]

Paralleling the revelations of "wisdom from above", this prophecy necessitates revolutionary discoveries occurring simultaneously in the secular world, the "wisdom from below". Stimulated by the Industrial Revolution of the 18th century, the wellsprings of theoretical models and new technology have incessantly burst forth. A wholly new paradigm of scientific thought and consciousness — is emerging. The year 1840 witnessed the emergence of electromagnetic theory, which in turn paved the way for the discovery of radio waves, telecommunications, television, computers, and the investigation of atomic energy, and the atomic bomb. New psychological and neurological descriptions of the brain, ethnopharmacology, black hole phenomenon, genetic engineering, lasers and holography, are more examples of the changes and ideas that have taken place in our generation. Of even greater significance has been the effect of the early 19th century breakthroughs of non-Euclidean geometry, which set the stage for the 20th century theories of Einstein's relativity, quantum mechanics and the search for the Unified Field Theory. Currently, under the name of "Super Strings", this theory is being proclaimed by leading physicists as an unmistakable genesis of a new physics. Most recently the scientific community and public at large are being initiated into a new world of fractal geometry, chaos theory, virtual reality and the ever accelerating neural network of the worldwide Internet.

According to the teachings of esoteric Judaism, all knowledge, both spiritual and material wisdom, originally coexisted in a seamless unity within a higher dimension. Together these two modes of wisdom comprised a larger, all-encompassing Universal Torah (Torah meaning "Instruction" or "Teachings"). A collapse, however, ensued in which the database of all knowledge split itself into "spiritual" and "material" planes of existence. Thus, we have the basis for the historical conflict between "religion" and "science". Yet, any given mystical or technological truth can only be one of two sides of the same puzzle. Thus, the material world is also a mode of spirituality, only externalized and concretized. Vice versa, the spiritual world is a mode of the material reality, only internalized and spiritualized.

The ultimate truth is not revealed through the supra-natural alone nor is it only discovered through scientific development it is more than both. Both forms of wisdom are destined to reunite. Perforce this is stimulating a worldwide paradigm shift in consciousness. These stages of global evolution are aspects of the Messianic Era that is central to the teachings of esoteric as well as traditional Judaism.

Our role in the re-unification of these two modes of wisdom, according to this doctrine, is achieved by matching the right tool with the right job. In other words, we must use the new maps, models and metaphors of the "wisdom from below" in order to grasp the "wisdom from above". In turn, the transcendent wisdom of the Torah will cast its light of clarity and direction upon the enchanting and often overpowering tools of science and technology.

Additionally, according to the redemption doctrine of the Talmudic Sage-Mystics (specifically but not exclusively, the Shklov school of the Gaon of Vilna), the Messianic Age cannot be fully ushered in until specific scientific "vessels" are redeemed and returned to their higher-dimensional roots in their corresponding "lights" of Torah. It is a Torah axiom that there is only "one surface" to reality; any given true discovery or accepted hypothesis in the New Sciences can only be the concave surface to its own convexity in Torah. When the two "sides" are isomorphically aligned with each other, then all factors being equal and at the right time and place, the external scientific model will actually be "absorbed" back into the light of the Supernal Torah, intensifying and fortifying the supernal light now from the "inside-out".[10]

According to the Talmudic Sage-Mystics, after thousands of years of travel, humanity has reached the final shore. Across this great ocean lies a new mode of consciousness and a new territory of reality, *Eretz haHayim* — the Land of the [true] Living. Yet, even now, as we stand upon this seashore of the final vestiges of earthly space and time there are strange and mind-boggling artifacts being washed ashore. Let us now reach into the sand and redeem one small item that has, embedded within it, the fractal-sparks of divinity fallen data from the higher-dimensional Tree of Knowledge. In so doing we can prepare ourselves to usher in a Messianic Era of higher dimensional consciousness. I believe one of these fallen fractal-sparks — more like a huge chunk — of divine data is the consciousness and medical knowledge now coming forth about a mysterious little organ in the middle of the brain known as the pineal gland, and DMT, an enigmatic substance produced within every human body. The light it sheds upon perhaps Judaism's greatest secret and gift to the world — the Foundation Stone — is truly revelatory and profoundly timely.

3. The Foundation Stone: Anyone Got a Light?

From their birth at Mt. Sinai over 3,300 years ago, the Jewish people as a nation have had an uncanny history of inexplicable unity as the Talmudic Sage-Mystics teach, "All of Israel are interconnected one with the other". Certainly, considering the relentless persecution, destruction and genocide they have suffered for millennia, there is virtually no comparison to the phenomenon of *Klal Yisrael* (the Collective Soul of Israel) throughout creation. On a very deep level the individuals that make up the Nation of Israel comprise a collective mind with a collective mission. What is that mission? For millennia numerous explanations have been put forth by traditional Jews, sectarian and assimilated Jews together with good intentioned gentiles as well as by bad intentioned anti- Semites with their infamous Jewish conspiracy theories. Nothing (outside of the unbroken tradition of the inner circles of the Talmudic Sage-Mystics until this day), however, accounts for the undeniably inexplicable and virtually supernatural facts on the table of history.

The existence of the Foundation Stone offers an unexpected, yet most ancient and profound answer. Using a modern metaphor, the current descendants of the Patriarchs and Matriarchs are the pilots of spaceship-earth. Under the guidance of the Supernal Emanator, and with their Torah as their map to creation, the Nation of Israel is about to take our current reality (known as "This

World") into the higher-dimensional Messianic Era and beyond (known as "The Next World"). The inner-spaceship of unified Jewish consciousness has everything it needs to take off and to fulfill its destined mission; all the supplies are onboard and all systems are "go". Most Jews in the world today, however, simply can't see the control panel of their own ship because someone simply needs to turn on the light for them. Although our sworn enemies are fast upon us and the spiritual geopolitical clock is forebodingly past the eleventh hour, there is still time to turn the lights on in the collective Jewish mind so it can awaken.

Is there a single "switch" to flick on to be found at the center of the collective Jewish people? What can so profoundly transform the some 13 million Jews in the world today and especially the 5.5 million Jews living in Israel? Aside from magical thinking and religious enthusiasm, is such a thing actually possible? Astoundingly it is. This secret switch has a history so primeval that it even precedes the birth of the Jewish Nation at Sinai. The "light switch" is called the *Even Shetiya* — the Foundation Stone, the Rock upon which Jacob had his dream-vision and upon which the Holy of Holies stood. It is the Foundation Stone that lies at the center of collective Jewish consciousness and it is longing in deep anticipation to be fully switched on. The Foundation Stone, along with being the greatest shield of protection and spiritual weaponry we have against Israel's enemies, is also the royal road to Torah consciousness.

The function of the Foundation Stone is ultimately the most profound secret in all of creation. It is the Jewish Nation's true national treasure and the time has now come for its secret to be revealed. There is something quite literally buried inside this ancient Foundation Stone waiting to be rediscovered and literally brought to light, as will be explained. Providentially, the full impact of the secret of the Foundation Stone could only be made known in our present generation. It is only in the last few decades that modern scientific research has offered us a model to understand that which previously only the prophets, the Talmudic sages and Kabbalists received through an unbroken transmission buttressed with *ruach hakodesh* and direct experience.

Jerusalem's Foundation Stone is presently encased and imprisoned in a large domed shrine constructed by invading Moslems from Arabia in the year 691 C.E. This shrine (although Moslems individually may pray there at times, it was not built nor is it used today as an actual mosque) is the Dome of the Rock. The rock under that dome is none other than the original Foundation Stone which was the bedrock upon which the Holy of Holies stood in the First and Second Temple! Its unique Jewish history, however, goes back even further — back to the very primeval beginnings of creation. According to the Talmudic Sage-Mystics, it was from this "rock" in a higher-dimension that the world was created, the rock being the first part of the Earth — both spiritual and physical[11]— to come into existence.[12] In the words of the Zohar[13], "The world was not created until the Holy One took a "stone" called *Even Shetiya* and threw it into the depths where it was fixed from above until below, and from it the world expanded. It is the center point of the world and on this spot stood the Holy of Holies". (*Even Shetiya* literally means The Weaving Stone, i.e., the primal substance from which all reality/consciousness was woven.)

The Foundation Stone is the summit of Mt. Moriah and the Talmud tells us that it was from this site that the Creator gathered the primeval earth that was formed into Adam. It was on this rock that Adam—and later Cain, Abel, and Noah—offered sacrifices to God. The Foundation Stone is the site of the Binding of Isaac where Abraham fulfilled God's test. This is the rock upon which Jacob laid his head and had his dream-vision of the angels ascending and descending a heavenly ladder. Upon awakening Jacob anointed the rock with a type of oil, the origin of which will become astoundingly clear as explained below.

The primeval roots, cosmic centrality, imminent revelation and future role of the Foundation Stone cannot be overstated. The historic and prophetic function of this geographical coordinate — and its spiritual correspondences — permeate the ancient prophetic and rabbinic traditions. Located at the intersection of Europe, Asia and Africa, the Land of Israel and Jerusalem were destined to be at the crossroads of civilization. Moreover, the sages repeatedly taught that, "Jerusalem is the center of the world". The center of Jerusalem was the Temple Mount, also known as Mt. Moriah from the time of Abraham. The center of the Temple was the Holy of Holies wherein rested the Ark of the Covenant containing within it the *original Aseret HaDibrot* (Ten Commandments). This wooden box overlaid in gold with its twin solid gold *keruvim* (cherubs) on top was itself resting upon an outcrop of bedrock known as the *Even Shetiya*, the Foundation Stone. King David and his son Solomon constructed the entire Temple around this specific space, having received the tradition that this was the very spot where Jacob dreamed, and where Isaac his father was bound along with the other chains of events that occurred there. They knew that this spot was a cosmic geographical vector point and that the rectification of all humanity and reality depended upon it being consciously utilized and directed.

Why were all these intense historical and spiritual activities taking place at this precise location? The Talmud explains that it was called the Foundation Stone because it was literally the foundation of the universe, the first point at which the Creator began weaving together the strands of divine light in proto-spacetime that would become creation.[14] In other words, the Foundation Stone is the higher-dimensional vortex — the axis mundi — wherein all worlds and dimensions of existence converge and intersect.[15] Here is where every particle of mass and every wave of energy — both spiritual and physical — are generated. Life comes in through this point and death leaves through this point. All earthly prayers are transmitted here and all divine flux flows into the world from here. This higher- dimensional portal is, ultimately, the corridor through which all consciousness — human and divine — passes. The Foundation Stone, as much as we are able to express that which we cannot express, is the very center of "God's Consciousness", the beginning point within the "Godhead". In the language of the Kabbalah, this is the point singularity of the *"tzimtzum"*, the paradoxical "contraction" (regression) that precedes the "expansion" (egression) of creation.[16] Regarding this non-dimensional "point" an ancient midrash states[17]:

16th century map depicting Jerusalem at the center of
the three continents of Europe, Asia and Africa[18]

As the navel is set in the center of the human body,
so is the land of Israel the navel of the world...
situated in the center of the world,
and Jerusalem in the center of the land of Israel,
and the Sanctuary in the center of Jerusalem,
and the holy place in the center of the Sanctuary,
and the Ark in the center of the holy place,
*and the **Foundation Stone** in the center of the holy place[19],*
because from it the world was founded.

Everything stated above about the Foundation Stone may sound intriguing. Ultimately, however, aren't these traditions about a magical-like "foundation stone" at the center of the world simply part of religious beliefs — Jewish "legends" that are not to be taken literally but rather have an allegorical or "mystical" meaning? Even if they are true, on whatever level of understanding, aside from being a Jewish historical "claim to title" to the Temple Mount, what relevance does the Foundation Stone have to us, *right here, right now*? And, in any event, there is a massive gilded shell — the Dome of the Rock — encasing the Foundation Stone that is under Moslem control. We are not advocating removing the dome in order to take the rock and the Temple Mount back into Jewish possession. With over a billion Moslems worldwide, that would surely spark WWIII — and then what? No, this is not at all the approach suggested here.

Truthfully, there is a battle to wage in this arena that, although much more covert, is even more powerful and astounding in its ramifications. Moreover, all supporters, friends and lovers of Israel can directly participate in this campaign without having to make a pilgrimage to the Holy Land. The challenge is not to remove the dome that is holding the spiritual essence of the Foundation Stone captive. Rather, all humanity has the innate emotional, spiritual and psychic ability to *implode* the Foundation Stone from the *inside out*. This can be achieved by methodically training our minds to "squeeze the rock" and release from it what has been dormant within it from its inception.[20] Something virtually "alien", quite literally out of this world and almost unimaginable is buried within the enigmatic Foundation Stone. The collective Jewish mind has an inborn ability to release the dormant power of the Foundation Stone, yet as explained below, virtually every man, woman and child can learn how to do it.

We should already suspect there is more going on with the Foundation Stone than meets the eye. This is obvious considering the fact of Jerusalem's geographical location and all the historical events that have taken place there as well as all the events prophesied to take place there. Truly, like the proverbial bull's eye, all eyes of the world have been and continue to be turned towards Jerusalem and the Temple Mount. The world may think that their historical and current obsession with this very small piece of property is simply a matter of politics, religion and nationalism, but this spot contains the world's most powerful secret — the actual center of collective human consciousness. Most importantly, the Foundation Stone may be the only emergency failsafe mechanism remaining to save Israel, ourselves and the world.

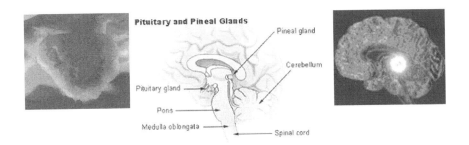

4. The Messianic Role of the Pineal Gland

There is an enigmatic endocrine organ located in the very middle of the human brain known as the pineal gland. It was given this name, meaning "pinecone like", in the beginning of the 18th century due to its anatomical resemblance to a pinecone. (It is pronounced variously as *pe-*, *pie-* and *pahy-* neal). This tiny gland, the smallest distinct organ in the entire human body, is about the size of a grain of rice. It also has the unique distinction as being the only organ in the brain that is singular in structure, i.e., it is not doubled by having right and left lobes as do all other organs in the brain. For millennia, it has been known in Oriental traditions to be the site referred to as the sixth or "third eye" chakra and/or to the seventh or "crown chakra".[21] In the Occidental tradition, the French philosopher, mathematician and physicist René Descartes (1596-1650) among others, had identified it as the "seat of the soul".

Relatively recently there has been discovered and synthesized a substance called dimethyltryptamine or DMT for short. It is one of the most powerful consciousness-altering chemical compounds known to science and it is naturally produced within the human body![22] DMT has also been found to exist within numerous animal and plant species as well. Essentially, everywhere science has so far investigated organic matter; either actual DMT or the chemical precursors that are necessary to manufacture DMT have been found. (From the perspective of using the DMT model to understand the function of the global Foundation Stone, this fact will be shown below to be very relevant). There is a new hypothesis that is gaining attention which asserts that additionally, DMT, under specific conditions, is generated in much greater quantities by the pineal gland. It is a fact that this organ manufactures the well-known hormone or neurotransmitter melatonin which affects our relationship to darkness and sleep. According to current thought, based upon new scientific studies and observation as well upon anecdotal and spiritual traditions, the pineal gland is also capable of manufacturing the mysterious substance DMT. The question is why and for what purpose?

Leading-edge professionals in fields such as psychiatry, chemistry and ethnopharmacology make the case that DMT released by the pineal gland enables the soul's movement in and out of the body and is an integral part of the birth and death experience as well as NDE's (Near Death Experiences). Recently, following a five year federally-supported study, one researcher hypothesized that when the pineal is stimulated under natural conditions, DMT has profound affects upon one's consciousness and experience of realty.[23] It has been proposed that during visionary and even during Biblical prophetic experiences, a significant amount of DMT is released by the pineal gland which facilitates the human interface with higher-dimensionality, alien worlds and the realm of the divine. Consequently, the type of molecule which in the pineal body produces this liquid hormone has been coined the "spirit molecule".

When it was first synthesized, DMT gained some limited experimentation in the late 1950's and 1960's. It has only gained prominence, however, in the last several decades and specifically in the last few years. A significant impetus to the growing popularity and fascination with DMT is that DMT is a major component in a South American brew called ayahuasca. Ayahuasca, with its own organically occurring DMT, has been used for spiritual and healing purposes for centuries by shamanic-based indigenous people of the

Western Amazon. A new tourist industry has developed in countries like Peru (where it is legal and its usage is actively supported by the government) with seekers coming primarily from North America and Europe. Consequently, the ritualistic usage of ayahuasca has spread to these continents. (It is reported that ritualistic group usage of ayahuasca has also become popular in Israel among primarily secular spiritual seekers). There are now numerous books, websites, documentaries, online videos, magazines, news articles, its own Facebook page and spiritually and scientific based groups devoted to understanding what this substance is, why the body naturally produces it and what can we learn from it. The effects of naturally occurring or synthetically produced DMT can be so inexplicably alien and other worldly that some investigators even suggest that the question that must be asked is "It is not so much what DMT is but what is the DMT spirit molecule trying to tell us".

From the perspective of the prophesied confluence between the ancient, esoteric Torah transmissions and the previously unimaginable discoveries and theories of the New Sciences, the tradition of the Talmudic Sage-Mystics also ask, "From a Torah perspective what can the new scientific and medical information about DMT tell us? In other words, what role in the redemption process, both collectively and personally, can the vessels of this phenomenon tell us about the truth and light concealed in the Torah? Can we use it as a scientific model to understand that which only the Kabbalah masters of former times knew and less encoded throughout their often bewildering and seemingly contradictory aggadic and midrashic statements? Can this scientific model now being born in our generation even shed light on obscure passages and practices found throughout Biblical scripture? Can this field of study be a "fractal chunk" in the prophetic messianic reunion of Kabbalah and science that is destined to precede and be part of the Messianic Age? I believe that the medical knowledge and the-

ories of consciousness now coming forth about the pineal gland
and its hypothesized role in the production of endogenous DMT
is a direct key into Judaism's greatest and most powerful secret —
the role and function of the *Even Shetiya* — the Jerusalem Foundation Stone.

From a Rabbinic and Kabbalistic perspective, a spiritual and
even prophetic role of the pineal gland and DMT concurs with the
Torah's understanding as to how, reality in general and the human body in particular, are constructed. As known in Torah, every "light" (in this case the higher-dimensional spirit aspect) requires its respective "vessel" (in this case the molecular neurotransmitter) to manifest itself in the world. It is written, "God created Man is His image" (Genesis 1:27). The Torah sages have always understood this formula to mean that the human body is a
detailed microcosm of the higher-dimensional divine "Image of
God".[24] Whatever exists in the human body must, ipso facto, have
its spiritual counterpart in the higher "heavenly'" dimension. Similarly, a verse from the Book of Job (19:26), "From my flesh I will
envision God." is regularly used by the Talmudic Sage-Mystics as
a proof-text formulating the cosmic principle that the human body
mirrors the higher-dimensional "Divine Body". Therefore, if the
pineal gland endogenously manufactures this extraordinary substance then it must have its corresponding analog in the divine
realm.

The human body is constructed with its exact physiology,
down to the smallest organs (e.g., the pineal body) and to the microscopic detail of the structure of our molecules (e.g., the DMT
molecule), precisely because the "divine body" is the primordial
root of these very structures. The physical body is isomorphic
with the divine body. Accordingly, we would have a pineal gland
in our brain capable of releasing significant amounts of DMT and
it would have the profound effects that it does precisely because

the divine "brain" has a higher dimensional analogous "pineal body". The corresponding "divine pineal body", under specific conditions, would also releases higher- dimensional DMT. "As above (and within), so below (and without)" and "As below, so above" are axiomatic in a Torah worldview. Additionally, there is a cosmic law that is fundamental to Torah scripture and the unbroken rabbinic tradition: All humanity together with the entire world are a single Adamic being with all the analogous parts and processes.

The human equivalent to a spiritually-based Foundation Stone is none other than the pineal body, which according to the new scientific hypothesis, plays a central role in human consciousness. This fact alone should not surprise us, as the subject of divine anatomy is well known in the Talmudic tradition and throughout Kabbalistic literature (as well as in Jewish philosophical thought). The correspondences between the divine body above and the human body below are axiomatic in the inner teachings of Judaism. Using knowledge from the new brain sciences, we can use the model of the physical pineal, and its surrounding structures and functions, as a vessel and lens to "see" into the secret of the metaphysical Foundation Stone. When one begins to put this correspondence into practice, learning to activate one's own pineal, concurrently with the higher-dimensional pineal, this experiential "knowing" is nothing less than revelatory and profoundly transformative. This is the beginning of true messianic consciousness as well as the ultimate shield and spiritual weapon against our enemies.

Now the question: If we consider the possibility of this being the case, what would be the higher-dimensional analog to the earthly DMT and where would its logical location be? The answer, utilizing the physiological pineal-DMT model, is evident. The existence of a spiritual DMT-like essence and the role of a corresponding divine "pineal- like" coordinate in the collective global brain in Torah tradition are fundamental. This phenomenon and its necessary role in the evolution and redemption of humanity have been known to the Talmudic Sage-Mystics for thousands of years. The existence of the pineal body and its crucial role in universal tikun (rectification) is well referenced (yet well concealed at the same time) throughout the Talmud, Midrash and Zohar and amplified through the two thousand year old written teachings of the Kabbalah (their oral transmission going back even further to Sinai, the Patriarchs and to Adam). The secret of a DMT-like "spiritual neurotransmitter" is known throughout Torah literature under various code-names and descriptions. One of the names of the universal pineal gland is the Foundation Stone. The geographical coordinate of the Foundation Stone is the Temple of Jerusalem, corresponding to the place of the higher-dimensional pineal gland in the collective mind of humanity — the "head" of Adam. The corresponding DMT-like liquid that it can manufacture and release throughout the body of humanity is the liquid light of universal consciousness. This is also known in the prophetic tradition as the "Living Liquid" *(Mayim Chayim)*. According to the ancient secret doctrine of the Talmudic Sage-Mystics the Living Liquid of global consciousness is now beginning to flow.

Before we continue a crucial point must be emphasized. The existence, the historical function and the future role of the Foundation Stone is not dependent upon our knowledge of the pineal gland. Nor is Jerusalem of the Mind dependent upon its hypostatized role in the production of endogenous DMT. Rather, it is the current model of the pineal organ and its role in consciousness that is important. Simply like a flashlight, the illumination alone that it shines upon this most ancient and crucial role of Jerusalem and the Foundation Stone is nothing less than messianic.

Moreover, even without the contemporary research into the

pineal organ and its current cultural fascination, based upon the multitude of traditions and secreted data from the Talmudic Sage-Mystics, the Torah would have eventually predicted a unique and pivotal role of the pineal body in human consciousness. As the microcosm (DMT and pineal research) sheds light on the macro-cosm (the cosmic role of Jerusalem and the *Even Shetiyah*) so does the macrocosm direct us to its own corresponding microcosm. Consequently, it is only a matter of time before the scientific truth regarding the pineal organ is verified simultaneously with the revelation of the spiritual truth of the secret of the Foundation Stone. Our tradition is *"Leka meday d'la remeza b'Oriata"* – "There is nothing that is not encoded into the Torah" (Talmud and Zohar).

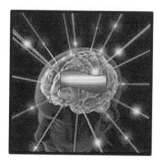

5. The River of Light: Global DMT

The forty-seventh chapter of Ezekiel describes a phenomenon of an unusual "river" of life-giving fluid appearing in the Holy of Holies — the Inner Sanctum — of a future Third Temple (Solomon's Temple, being the first, was destroyed in 586 BCE and "Herod's Temple" being the second, was destroyed in 70 CE):

> The [angelic] man brought me back to the entrance of the temple, and I saw "water" coming out from under the threshold [beneath the entrance to the Holy of Ho- lies, i.e., the Foundation Stone] of the temple toward the east (as the temple faced east).

In his corresponding vision of the higher-dimensional future Jerusalem, the prophet Joel (4:18) describes,

> And all the springs of Judah will flow with liquid (*may- im*) and a well-spring from the House of HaShem [i.e., Jerusalem and/or the Temple and/or the Holy of Holies] will go out... .

Similarly, and more well known, the prophet Zechariah prophesizes (14:8-9),

It shall be on that day, living liquid (*Mayim Chayim*) will flow out of Jerusalem... . The Name/Formula ("Lord") will be the King over the entire world; on that day The Lord will be One and His Name will be One.

Concerning the transformative properties of this unusual substance Rabbi Moshe Chayim Luzzatto (Ramchal), one of the greatest Talmudic Sage-Mystics of the 18th century wrote[25], "This [liquid] is not the same as the basic sustenance given to enable all things to subsist [i.e., water], but rather it is a superior and precious light that comes out from the Holy of Holies". In other words, it is only referred to as "water" because it has certain characteristics akin to water including being the most basic and sustaining element of life, but not because it consists of hydrogen and oxygen, the elements that make up earthly water.[26]

The Hebrew word "*mayim*" does mean water but it also refers to any liquid or liquid-like substance (e.g., "watery" in English). Even aside from Ramchal's explanation above, from the descriptions given in the words of the prophets concerning this Living Liquid, we are clearly not talking about any kind of earthly "water", i.e., that constitutes some 97% of our physical bodies as well as most of the surface of this planet. We can also assume that the "world's waterways" referred to in the same prophetic passages describing a future Third Temple are also not what they would appear to be. Rather, this liquid-like substance is of a higher-dimensional origin. The Living Liquid is the medium and the carrier of super- consciousness itself.[27]

That this "liquid" is pure, Godly consciousness is evident from a well-known verse in Isaiah (55-12), "You shall draw waters joyously from the wells of salvation". Quoting this verse and in direct connection to the new "river of the future", the Talmud teaches that, in fact, it is not "water" at all that is being drawn from the future "wells of salvation"! Rather, the Talmudic Sage-Mystics explicitly state that it is *ruach hakodesh* — lit., "sacred spirit" — that begins trickling out from the floor of the Holy of Holies, the Foundation Stone. When we interface *mayim*/water with *ruach*/spirit, this substance reveals itself as a numinous Living Liquid, bubbling and rising up from beneath the Holy of Holies. This higher-dimensional substance is also known as the *Ohr Ha-Ganuz*, the Hidden Light, higher-dimensional messianic consciousness. This will be the beginning of the fulfillment of the prophet Joel (3-1), "And it will be in the end of days, I will pour out My *ruach*/spirit upon all flesh, and your sons and daughters shall prophesize; your elders shall dream dreams, your young men shall see visions".[28] This *ruach*/spirit is the Living Liquid, the higher-dimensional equivalent to the release of "universal DMT".

The Talmud also teaches that at a future time (i.e., the higher-dimensional messianic state of reality) the stream of water that was channeled by aqueducts in the First and Second Temples would be replaced by one coming naturally out of the Holy of Holies sitting atop the Foundation Stone. This is strange because there never has been any natural source of water on the Temple Mount. Moreover, we are told that in the Messianic Era this small stream will become a mighty torrent of spiritual blessing for the "waterways" of all mankind. Upon these verses the master Talmudic Sage-Mystic the Gaon of Vilna (1720-1797) comments: "The water which, in the Second Temple, flowed out through the water gate in a trickle [via aqueducts], will one day have its source in the Holy of Holies and issue from under the threshold of the House [the Holy of Holies]". This is the higher-dimensional liquid light of the Living Liquid flowing out to all humanity from the Foundation Stone, our collective "pineal gland".

There are numerous other parallels between the human pineal gland and the Jerusalem Foundation Stone (more of which is explained below). Each one, pineal of the body and Peniel of Jerusalem, informs upon the other, enabling one's understanding of both phenomena to mutually evolve. The geographical Foundation Stone is the macrocosm to the microcosmic physiological pineal. The relationship maintains its ratio, there always being two polarities and two terminals. As the collective Jerusalem above, so the personal Jerusalem below. As Jerusalem of the Mind is within each of us, so is the geographical Jerusalem the mind of the world. Torah teaches a fundamental principle: every human being has within his or her cranium a complete "model" version of a neurological Jerusalem, with a Temple Mount, a Holy of Holies, an Ark of the Covenant and *keruvim* resting atop of a Foundation Stone. Every human being has not only a "temple within" but Torah teaches us that we also have a microcosmic *Even Shetiya* within us that is capable of releasing a personal and universal liquid light of consciousness. Now, the question is what do we do with it?

The symmetry and fractal formulation (i.e., a pattern iterating self-similar versions of itself yet each one utterly unique from every other one), between the "upper" (external) geopolitical Foundation Stone and the "lower" (internal) Foundation Stone of the Mind is self-evident. As mentioned, deeper exploration of the relationship between the two reveals an array of additional similarities. There is one correlation of self-similarity, however, that is impossible to overlook as it is staring us in the "face", quite literally. As mentioned, the Foundation Stone and its adjacent locations on Mount Moriah and the Temple structures constructed there, have many biblical appellations, rabbinic cognomens and Kabbalistic code names, each one emphasizing different aspects. Another Biblical and Kabbalistic name for the vortex centered in the Foundation Stone is *Peniel*. This term, transliterated from the Hebrew (pronounced either as *p'nee-el* or *p'nay-el*), literally means "Face" or "Presence of God". Following Jacob's nocturnal battle with an angelic entity, upon the rising of the early morning light,

Scripture records (Genesis 32-24, 30), "So Jacob called the name of the place Peniel, saying, "For I have seen God face to face... ".[29] *Pineal, please meet Peniel.*

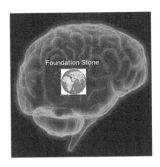

6. P2P: The Peniel Principle

A perennial enigma that has perplexed much of the world — both gentiles and Jews — is the question of the "choseness" or "speciality" of the Jewish people. The spectrum of responses has ranged from one end of the spectrum to the other — and then some. From the perspective of Jerusalem of the Mind the resolution to this riddle is both profoundly simple and simply profound. The fundamental purpose of Torah and the Jewish Nation is to help direct all humanity — including the Jews themselves — towards one immutable cosmic law: The world, together with the entirety of humanity, is literally one collective consciousness existing within one collective human-like form. This "super soul-body" is the higher-dimensional Adam (containing both masculine and feminine) that has undergone an unfathomable dimensional collapse (the "Fall"). According to most contemporary Torah authorities the original Adamic consciousness is in the process of resurrecting itself along with the entirety of his higher-dimensional reality. The resurrected Adam, as known in the tradition of the Talmudic Sage-Mystics, is none other than the Messiah himself and the return to his rectified reality and original consciousness is the period known as the Messianic Era. This process begins in the center of his Peniel consciousness, the geographical Jerusalem Foundation Stone, the higher-dimensional corollary to our physiological pineal body.

There are numerous paths that lead into the global pineal, but they all have in common the formula P2P, i.e., oscillating back and forth between the two "P's" — the anatomical pineal and the geographical Peniel. Together they reveal something more than both.

Before we introduce the P2P equation two crucial points must be emphasized. Dimethyltryptamine is not a person, place or thing. It does not possess its own sentient consciousness. It is not a spirit to be allotted any unique status. It is simply a transmitter. It has been called the "spirit molecule" not because it is some form of a spirit, but rather because it facilitates communication—in the broadest sense of the word—between the physical and the spiritual, between our material, everyday reality and a higher-dimensional, non-ordinary reality. DMT, whether produced endogenously within the body, derived from plant matter or produced synthetically, in and of itself does not do anything. The chemical and molecular composition of this naturally occurring substance unlocks an interface into parallel, free-standing yet intersecting dimensions. It is only a key to the door, not what is on the other side of the door.

This is essentially what all the chemicals and neurotransmitters involved with our senses and thought processes in our brain do. DMT, however, appears to be the chemical "mother" of all the cerebral- neurological processes involved with consciousness. DMT opens certain circuits within the brain that allows us to see and experience everyday reality—or what we thought was everyday reality—from an extremely different and otherworldly inner perspective. It is DMT's overall effect on human consciousness and its strongly suspected connection to the pineal gland that is being used as a model to understand the enigmatic nature of the Foundation Stone.

Furthermore, Jerusalem of the Mind is not interested in DMT itself (or in any of its pharmacological siblings and relatives in the tryptomine family). In using it as a model to begin to unravel the ancient Jewish mystery of the Foundation Stone we are not interested per se in the specific encounters that have and continue to be reported of alien beings, alien worlds, NDE experiences or even traumatic reassessments of reality and of one's purpose in life. The specific clinical and ritual accounts of DMT and ayahuasca are a valuable study in and of themselves, but the observations and conclusions of what these experiences mean and how they can be of benefit to us are also not of direct concern here. Rather, in the tradition of the probing interdisciplinarian mind and zealous mission of the Talmudic Sage-Mystic, it is the recent astounding discovery of the DMT-pineal model with its physiological and theoretical ramifications that are of keen interest. In fact, this model appears to be an actual key to open the doors of Torah perception and reveal to our dazed and confused global consciousness a real and tangible light at the end of the tunnel.[30]

The four-point formulation or "Peniel Principle" below is simple and compelling in its iterating fractal symmetry, i.e., its micro-macro self-similarity:

1a. Located in the center of the brain is an enigmatic little organ (relative to the other organs in the brain and the surrounding limbs of the body) known as the pineal gland that is the subject of remarkable new scientific exploration.

1b. Located in the center of the world is an enigmatic little rock (relative to the other rocks and mountains and the surrounding nations of the world) known as the Foundation Stone that is the subject of remarkable ancient Jewish traditions.

~~~

2a. Historically, the pineal body has been associated both in the Orient and in the Occident with different functions of consciousness including being the seat of the human soul through which spirit enters and leaves.

2b. Historically, the Foundation Stone has been associated in the Bible, Talmud and kabbalistic traditions with different functions of global consciousness including being the "seat" of the world's collective soul and through which the world's spirit enters and leaves.

~~~

3a. Until now, however, there has been no mechanistic model or physiological explanation as to how it functions and why the human body even needs a pineal gland centered in the brain, the consciousness center of the body.

3b. Until now, however, there has been no mechanistic model or metaphysical explanation as to how it actually functions and why the collective world body even needs a Foundation Stone centered in Jerusalem, the consciousness center of the world.

~~~

4a. It is now theorized that the pineal gland is capable of generating a natural substance known as Dimethyltryptamine (DMT), an extraordinarily powerful essence that is able to alter one's personal consciousness, transport a person's mind into an inner metaphysical dimension and imprint one with a radical life-changing spiritual experience.

4b. It has long been known that the Foundation Stone is capable of generating a universal substance known as *Mayim Chayim* — "Living Liquid", an extraordinarily powerful liquid light essence that is able to alter our collective consciousness, transport humanity's mind into an inner metaphysical dimension and imprint all of us with a radical world-changing Godly experience.

The operative mechanism of the Peniel Principle is, in part, built upon the physics of resonance (also referred to as harmonics or entrainment). Resonance phenomena occur with all types of vibrations or waves such as mechanical resonance, acoustic resonance, electromagnetic resonance and others forms. The shattering of a crystal wineglass when exposed to a musical tone of the right pitch (its resonance frequency) is an example of acoustic resonance. The Torah's Peniel Principle informs us that the pineal body within our brains shares a minute fractured fraction (i.e., fractal) of the same frequency as the global pineal — the Foundation Stone. As explained above, Torah is teaching that every human being is an entire world unto itself complete with a "miniature" temple, covenantal ark and foundation stone within each and every cranium. By consciously activating one's pineal body and directing that resonating energy to the geographical pineal — the Jerusalem Foundation Stone — a dynamic feedback loop is generated. This is the formula P2P — pineal to ("2"=to) Peniel and then back again ("2", i.e., a second time), Peniel to pineal.

The P2P Peniel Principle is formulated to be used as a consciousness tool or "thought experiment" interfacing the human pineal with the higher-dimensional Peniel. This is an extremely powerful yet simple form of ancient Jewish prayer/meditation. In fact, the synergistic unification of so many disparate parts, e.g., science and Kabbalah, mind and consciousness, particular and collective, physical and metaphysical, local and non-local, DMT and the Living Liquid, etc. is quintessentially "Jewish". This is a goal of true Torah-based Judaism — unifying the two extremes of the particular and the universal. Used regularly and systematically, the dynamic of toggling back and forth between the two coordinates opens up an inter-dimensional tunnel or corridor. It then leads from one's personal Foundation Stone within the Jerusalem of the Mind directly to the universal geographical Foundation Stone of a reunited and singular humanity — the return to the original higher- dimensional Adam.

The Peniel Principle reveals to us that the two Foundation Stones are inextricably interconnected — they are iterating fractals of each other. Together they form a continuous feedback loop. The objective of this meditative prayer is, in affect, to "rub" one "stone" against the other, just as if we were rubbing one rock against another rock in order to create a spark to ignite a fire. Each one of us can use our individual pineal — our internal Foundation Stone to rock the universal Foundation Stone from the *inside out.* More specifically, the goal is to emotionally, mentally and psychically "squeeze" the rock so that its celestial liquid may begin to trickle out.

The Foundation Stone is currently imprisoned beneath the Dome of the Rock. Stimulating the Foundation Stone with our conscious thoughts of petitionary prayer and directed meditation can literally awaken it from its current "calcified", "atrophied" and "petrified" state and cause its river of liquid light to begin to seep. Concurrently, the collective mind of the Nation of Israel will begin to wake up and reclaim its dormant power and God-mandated mission. This is truly to "pray for the peace of Jerusalem" by reconnecting the severed "pieces". This is the true peace and it will only manifest when we interconnect the "pieces" of the micro-Jerusalem within ourselves with the macro-Jerusalem of the world and then back again. This is true, action-oriented "Jerusalem prayer". The Peniel Principle is the Royal Road to Torah Consciousness and the New Jerusalem as well as our sword and shield, personally and collectively, on the battlefront of both the physical and spiritual wars being waged against us.

~~~

We are now prepared to resolve the Talmudic riddle introduced above concerning the apparent contradiction between a celestial Jerusalem and an earthly Jerusalem. The Talmud states, "The Holy One said, 'I will not enter the Celestial Jerusalem (i.e., a higher-dimensional reality) until I enter the earthly Jerusalem (our lower- dimensional reality)'". This statement, as often the case, is a very terse formula of the Talmudic Sage-Mystics. According to the ancient tradition of Talmudic logic, hermeneutics and methodology, a formula of this nature must be applicable in all possible scenarios in order for it to be true. In this sense it is akin to a mathematical equation defining a law of physics. If an exception to the rule is found then the equation is not true and the mathematician or theoretician must go back to the drawing board.

This expression of the Talmudic Sage-Mystics, like many of the thousands that have been transmitted and encoded in the Talmud and Midrash, is a formula first and a statement only second. It is primarily defining the underlying cosmology that this transmission is predicated upon. In other words, in this case it must even be true in the face of the apparently opposing tradition that a third temple structure will first manifest by "descending" from "heaven", i.e. from a higher-dimension before it can manifest from below in our lower dimensionality. In Talmudic logic it is always assumed (unless there are extremely compelling reasons) that each rabbinic transmitter of a formula/statement is acutely aware of every other formula/statement made by all his predecessors as well as all those made by his colleagues in that generation of sage-masters.

If this is the case, then according to its own methodology, in order for this formula to be true, does it 1) require the actual construction of a physical Temple "below" and, does it 2) contradict the equally authoritative sources that appear to require the Temple to descend from "above"? According to the synergistic P2P equation the resolution is obvious and the logic is clear: God "enters" the Jerusalem of the Mind from below specifically through the human effort of "building" a network of interfacing earthly pineal bodies, microcosmic fractals of the Earthly Jerusalem. This collective DMT stimulation then enables the Divine Mind to enter the Heavenly Jerusalem causing the Jerusalem on High to descend below. One is the vessel and precursor for the light and conclusion of the other. Our collective network of inner Foundation Stones becomes a virtual global "docking station" for the higher-dimensional Foundation Stone to land, as it were. The Holy One has now "entered" both the upper Jerusalem and the lower Jerusalem via the fact that we have "entered" and stimulated our inner Jerusalem.[31] This accords with the well-known Torah axiom that, "There can be no radiating from Above that is not preceded by arousal from below".

Both the collective higher-dimensional Jerusalem and our personal human pineal Jerusalem act reciprocally upon each other. They are "looped in" to each other and continually "enlighten" each other. Each one "turns on" the other, creating an inter-global feedback loop. When we enter our own Foundation Stone of pineal consciousness we are, spark by spark and drop by drop, creating a "space" for the Divine to enter *us*, thus allowing for the Divine to enter the collective Foundation Stone of Peniel consciousness. This is literally the Light of Messianic Consciousness also known as the *Ohr Ganuz*. Accordingly, this is the intention of the formula, "The Holy One vowed that He will not enter the Celestial Jerusalem until He enters the earthly Jerusalem".

7. Jacob's Heavenly Oil

We are now prepared to unlock another door that the P2P formula opens up for us that was mentioned above. This is concerning the nature of the oil that Jacob poured upon a rock following his prophetic dream-vision. Genesis (28:10-22) records,

> Jacob left Beer Sheva and headed toward Charan. He en- countered *the place* and spent the night there, because the sun had set; he took of the stones of *the place* and arranged them about his head and lay down to sleep in *that place.* He had a vision in a dream and behold, a ladder was set upon the earth and its top reached heavenward; and behold! Angels of God were ascending and descending upon it [or upon Jacob]. Behold, God was standing over him and said, "I am YHVH, God of Abraham your father, and God of Isaac—the land upon which you lie—I will give you and your descendants... Jacob awoke from his sleep and said, "Indeed God is in *this place* and I was unaware". He became alarmed and he said, "How awesome is *this place,* it can only be the House of God and this is the gate of the heavens". Jacob arose early in the morning and took the stone that he had placed around his head and set it up as a pillar; then he poured oil on

its top". He named the place Bet El (House of God or God's Temple). The town's original name, however, had been Luz.

What is the significance of God as *Makom*? Our sages tell us that, "He is the place of the world *(Makom)* but the world is not His place", i.e., everything is contained within the Divine but the Divine is not contained within the world.[32]

The imagery of Jacob's ladder reaching up into the heights of the heavens with angelic beings ascending and descending upon it is one of the most pivotal events in cosmic history and contains the purpose and mission of *Klal Yisrael*. Unraveling the coded language of these verses requires an entire book. Here we will concern ourselves with only two points — the place where this phenomenon took place and the origin of the anointing oil. Regarding the "ladder" and its angelic forces, suffice it to say that, even according to the simple narrative, the ladder and the angles were taking place *within* Jacob himself, as it states, "Behold, angels of God were ascending and descending upon [i.e., within] him".[33]

Where was the location of Jacob's vision taking place? As is well known, that spot was the summit of Mount Moriah where the future Temples would be built. Specifically, he spent the night with his head resting on the very outcrop of rock atop Mount Moriah known as the *Even Shetiyah* (where the *Akeidah*—the Binding of Isaac—had occurred with his father and grandfather Abraham). What is the textual indication that this is so? The verse does not state that he alighted upon a place, but rather, "He alighted upon the Place" where place is prefixed with the definite article, i.e., *the* Place. What is *the* Place? The Place *(Makom)* is one of the many appellations or additional names for HaShem (HaShem itself meaning The Name that is the root of all His other names and aspects).

What is the significance of God as *Makom*? Our sages tell us that, "He is the Place (*Makom*) of the world but the world is not His place", i.e., everything is contained within the Divine but the Divine is not contained within the world. In other words, The Place is the very Foundation Stone itself. Jacob is entering into direct unification with the Divine and affecting a *tikun* there for all of future Israel, namely opening up the very vortex where lower and higher-dimensionality—"earth and heaven"—converge. "This is the Gate (or vortex) of Heaven", he declared. The pineal gland, as explained above, has long been considered the physiological nexus where the soul enters and leaves the body. It is a virtual microcosmic Foundation Stone.

Additionally, the Talmudic Sage-Mystics tell us that the origin of the oil that Jacob poured upon the *Makom*/Foundation Stone did not come from Jacob as he was not carrying any oil with him at that time. Rather, this "oil" flowed from a higher dimension ("*shamayim*/heaven"). When we realize that his head was literally in direct physical contact with the *Even Shetiyah*, the nature of this otherworldly oil becomes startlingly clear. According to the understanding of the P2P Principle, the "oil" dripping from "heaven" is literally the higher-dimensional analog to what science is beginning to understand and theorize about human DMT. It is the Living Liquid of the Hidden Light that Jacob was "opening" up at this coordinate in the higher-dimensional body of Adam. He was rectifying and preparing this very place for his great, great grandchildren—us—to continue the *tikun* he began and to erect there the Temples. It was being generated by Jacob in this spot from whence the global DMT flows.[34] (The additional significance that it was the back of his head is explained below in the secret of the Western Wall).

The Pineal Principle of Jerusalem of the Mind offers a far-reaching and literally messianic (i.e., futuristic/higher-dimensional) synthesis between that which is "man made" from below and that which is "God revealed" from above. By consciously stimulating and activating the individual pineal gland residing within each one of us — a literal microcosmic Foundation Stone — together we can stimulate and activate the collective "pineal gland" residing within Mount Moriah, the Temple Mount. *If we build it, it will come.* As each one of us builds his and her neurological inner-Temple this begins releasing the microscopic molecules of endogenous DMT. Then by directing one's thought to the geographical Foundation Stone, this will cause the collective Foundation Stone to begin releasing its analogous microscopic "spirit molecules" of *Mayim Chayi*m. This is the Living Liquid of the messianic river of divine consciousness that goes out to the "waterways" of the entire world. This is our secret "weapon" against our enemies as the *Mayim Chayim* has the power to transform the consciousness of even the most rabid anti- Semites and enemies of the God of Israel, if only by melting away the *klipot*/shells and spiritual virus that have possessed them.

8. The Geography of Prayer: What is Halachah?

Even though the concept and practice of Jerusalem of the Mind may initially appear very novel, all the sources quoted (in addition to the scientific data), are supported on the bedrock of Talmud, Midrash, Zohar and the unbroken transmission of the Kabbalah. Yet, truly there is nothing novel being presented here. To the contrary, as is known, every Jew is obligated to make Jerusalem, the Temple's remaining wall (the Kotel) and the Foundation Stone the center of his or her consciousness. King David in his Psalms is explicit:

> *If I forget you, O Jerusalem,*
> *let my right hand forget its skill.*
> *Let my tongue cling to my palate*
> *if I fail to recall you,*
> *If I fail to elevate Jerusalem*
> *above my highest joy.*[35]

Specifically during *tefilah*/prayer, the Code of Jewish Law (*Shulchan Aruch*), quoting the Talmud, requires us to focus and actually project our consciousness into the envisioned Holy of Holies constructed upon the bedrock of the Foundation Stone. Within the laws of prayer R' Yoseph Caro writes:

> When one stands up to pray [the silent *amidah*], if he is in the Diaspora he should turn his face towards *Eretz Yisrael*. He should also direct his thought to Jerusalem, to the [location of the] Temple and to the *Kodesh HaKedoshim* (the Holy of Holies). If one is standing in *Eretz Yisrael* he should turn his face towards Jerusalem and he should also direct his thought to Jerusalem, to the Temple and to the *Kodesh HaKedoshim*. If one is standing in Jerusalem he should turn his face towards the Temple and also to the *Kodesh HaKedoshim*.[36]

This is the universally excepted halacha/law to the extent that if one is praying at the Kotel one must also turn the body slightly at an angle to the left, and not directly towards the Kotel, so as to then be pointing in the direction of the Foundation Stone. This also explains, if one notices, why observant Jews praying the silent Standing Prayer at the Kotel are turning a bit to the left, i.e., towards the Foundation Stone that lies at the core of the Holy of Holies.[37] (However, as explained below, if one has entered through the Western Wall tunnel and is now facing directly across from the Foundation Stone [which is some 300 feet away at about a 45% angle] then one stands facing completely eastward). The authoritative *Mishnah Berurah*[38] (commentary on the Shulchan Aruch by R' Yisrael Meir Kagan, the *"Chofetz Chayim"*, 1838-1933) clarifies that, "One should direct his heart even in a circumstance where he cannot turn his face towards them (*Eretz Yisrael*, Jerusalem, the Temple or the Holy of Holies). ["Directing his heart"] means that one should concentrate with his emotions and thoughts as if he is standing in the Temple in Jerusalem in the [actual] place of the Holy of Holies".

In other words, the state of consciousness that one develops while practicing the intentions and methodology put forth in Jerusalem of the Mind, is simply what is required to be actively doing in any case. This applies whether one is in prayer, in meditation, in study or play, whether in pain, in pleasure, in sorrow or in ecstasy. From this perspective, all that is being offered here is a systematic approach and a series of mental and spiritual techniques to actually and literally make Jerusalem and the Foundation Stone the center of our consciousness *at all times and under all circumstances*. As our tradition explicitly states, to embrace the bedrock of Jewish consciousness is to embrace Jerusalem consciousness; the center of Jerusalem is the Foundation Stone from where emanates the consciousness and very existence of all humanity and creation. This is the "geography of prayer" and we only have to align our consciousness with the geo-center of global consciousness — the Foundation Stone.

The earthly and heavenly DMT released in Jerusalem of the Mind has many virtues and *tikunim* on many levels. Just in terms of prayer/*davening*, however, one of the greatest challenges for every observant Jew, from the *ba'al teshuvah* to the *rosh yeshiva*, from the *ba'al habayit* to the *talmid chacham*, is keeping *tefilah* fresh and alive three times daily, seven days a week, year in and year out. It is no secret that too many Torah-based Jews have essentially abandoned hope of ever discovering real and evolving spiritual excitement in their daily prayers if not actually having become lax in its regular performance. Jerusalem of the Mind and the exercises described here are virtually guaranteed to alter not only one's consciousness, but also one's daily *davening*. Although developing pineal/Peniel consciousness can be practiced any time and almost anywhere, if one incorporates the simple techniques into one's *tefilah*, as many have attested, the results can be nothing less than astounding.

Jerusalem of the Mind is the true and high road for every Jew as we are exhorted and mandated by King David down through the living chain of the Talmudic Sage-Mystics to the Shulchan

Aruch until this day. Training one's self to stay centered in the Jerusalem of the Mind is the royal road to Jewish consciousness, to Torah consciousness and the return to universal higher-dimensional Adamic consciousness. Making Jerusalem of the Mind a daily practice is to take seriously the responsibility to "grow one's own consciousness" as well as to become a conscious and participating member of the body of Israel. This methodology enables every Jew to actively become a fighting soldier in God's army battling and defending the honor and the very life of *Eretz Yisrael* and *Klal Yisrael*. Moreover, persistently training ourselves to "squeeze the rock", both in the center of our own brain and in the center of humanity, is to prepare our mind and body, as well as that of the world's collective mind and body, for the imminent Messianic Era and beyond.

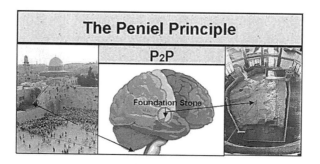

9. Between a Wall and a Hard Place

The *Kotel HaMa'aravi* (the Western Wall or simply the *Wall*, known among some gentiles as the "Wailing Wall") is universally recognized as Judaism's most sacred site. The Kotel, at the foot of the Temple Mount (Mt. Moriah), is a remnant of a massive retaining wall that buttressed and extended the platform of the Temple compound on its western bank. The Kotel has been a site for Jewish prayer and pilgrimage for centuries, being virtually the sole remnant of the Temple that remained, following its destruction by the Romans.[39] Thousands of Jews, as well as tourists from around the world, pray and visit daily at the Kotel. Every year on Tisha B'Av large crowds congregate at the Wall to commemorate the destruction of the Temple. On the Ninth of Av in 2007 over 100,000 gathered at the Wall.[40] During the month of Tishrei (containing the festivals of Rosh HaShanah, Yom Kippur and Sukkot — August/ September) 2009, a record 1.5 million people visited the site.[41]

Although the Kotel, for almost 2,000 years has been sacred to Jews as a site of prayer and mourning, over the last several centuries the Kotel has become central to Jewish consciousness, not only for religious but for secular Jews as well. Following the recapture of eastern Jerusalem in 1967, a large plaza in front of the Kotel was created which is used regularly for worship and public gatherings, including Bar Mitzvah celebrations and the swearing-in ceremonies for soldiers in the Israel Defense Forces. Every dignitary and public notable visiting Israel visits the Wall. More than a million prayer notes are placed in the cracks and crevices of the Wall each year.[42]

As sacred and central as the Kotel is in Jewish consciousness, the underlying reason for its holiness and centrality is often overlooked. As noted, it is only a retaining wall for the Temple compound (not a wall of the Temple itself). What has imbued the location of the Kotel with its unique status is that it has been the closest accessible point to the true holiest spot in Judaism, namely the Foundation Stone. It is the Kotel's proximity to the Holy of Holies that has given the Kotel its status. This is evident in that Jewish Law dictates that when a Jew prays the *amidah*/standing silent prayer, the deciding factor of which direction one ultimately faces is not the Kotel but the Foundation Stone.

Therefore, the Mishnah states that, of all the four walls of the Temple Mount, the Western Wall was the closest to the Holy of Holies[43] and, to pray by the Wall is particularly beneficial. As one walks along the Western Wall through the tunnel that is now accessible, there will shortly appear a sign on the Wall that informs you that you are now standing:

"Opposite the Foundation Stone
and the Site of the Holy of Holies"

As with virtually everything in Jewish history (as well as in world history), nothing happens randomly. The existence of the Kotel is certainly no exception as Divine providence ordained that it would never be destroyed. Originally, upon conquering Jerusalem the Roman general Vespasian (who was to become Emperor, Titus taking his place) ordered the destruction of the Temple. He assigned the destruction of the four walls surrounding the Temple complex to his four generals. Pangar, the Duke of Arabia [!], was ordered to destroy the Western Wall. Pangar, however, did not destroy the wall because, "It had been decreed by Heaven that the western wall should never be destroyed because the Shechinah — God's Presence — dwells in the west". When asked by Vespasian why he did not destroy it, Pangar replied that he intentionally did not destroy it so that it would stand as an eternal sign of what Vespasian had conquered. Although the Emperor acknowledged that he did, in fact, make a good decision, but because he did not follow his original order he was duly executed.[44]

The principle of an additional level of *kedusha* associated with a westward direction is well known in Jewish tradition. The human form has spiritual directions built into it. The face (and the front of the body) are always one's "east" and the back of the head (and the back of the body) are always one's west (One's left side is the north and the right side is the south). The Shechinah—God's Presence— "dwells" in the west whether one's relative geographical west or one's "bodily" west. It is for this reason, for example, that on Friday night in the synagogue when welcoming in the Shabbat bride, the congregation turns specifically to the west to greet Her. One's back, being one's "west" side, also defines the directions one turns during the ritual of "shaking" the Lulav during Sukkot.[45]

There is something, however, deeply relevant about the Kotel's association with the Shechinah's "dwelling in the west" that is more than religious nostalgia. Another example of this principle sheds an unexpected light upon the function and higher-dimensional coordinates of the Kotel and its relationship to the Foundation Stone. This little known Torah detail reveals a spiritual secret that quite literally opens up a hidden "corridor" or circuit between a wall—the Kotel—and a hard place—the Foundation Stone.

The back of the head is one's bodily west therefore the Shechinah dwells in the back of the head. The "west" and back of the head of a person is also the location of the mysterious "luz bone", a type of inter-dimensional coordinate from which one's true eternal body(s) and soul(s) are "reconstituted" at the time of the great Resurrection (i.e., the point of intersection between *"Olam HaZeh"* and *"Olam HaBah"*, i.e., the reunion of lower and higher-dimensionality). Consequently, the Western Wall, where the Shechinah dwells, is the outline of a giant, cosmic "luz bone" from which the higher- dimensional Temple of Adamic consciousness will also be resurrected. Just as the pineal gland is one's personal Foundation Stone, if the Wall is the "back of the "head" of the Temple structure, then the Foundation Stone, relative to the Wall, can only be the spiritual "pineal gland" with its associative higher-dimensional Adamic DMT! This, as mentioned above, is the secret behind the *halachah* of the "geography of prayer" — to simply align one's consciousness along the spiritual east-west axis of the Foundation Stone and the Western Wall.

When a person dies, the various levels of the soul (*chaiyah, neshamah, ruach*), return to their respective extra-dimensional roots. The lowest level of the soul, the *nefesh*, remains with the corpse until the body decays and disintegrates. The *nefesh* then also returns to its source leaving only the bones in the grave. There remains, however, a field of dormant life-energy that "sleeps" with the bones and never departs. This force, in the language of the Talmudic Sage-Mystics, is known as "*havla degarmay*", "vapor of the bones" and it is from this "vapor of the bones" that the soul, together with the body, are "cloned", as it were, back into its original, and now perfected, state. Ramchal writes[46]:

> There remains in the grave of a person a bone which is called "luz". Through it the body will be reconstructed at the time of the resurrection of the dead. There also remains [in the bone(s)] a portion of the *nefesh* which is called "the vapor of the bones". Likewise, in the case of the Temple there remains the Western Wall.

Within the Western Wall tunnel facing eastward you are now about 300 feet from the actual Foundation Stone. However, you are not level with the Foundation Stone as the platform of Mount Moriah with the outcrop of the *Even Shetiya* (covered by the Dome of the Rock) reaches far above you. If you stretch a direct line between you and the Foundation Stone you would be looking up at about a 45 degree angle. Amazingly, but not surprisingly, this angle is approximately the same 45 degrees from the back of the head the area of the Luz bone — to the pineal gland in the middle of your brain! This area, at the indentation of the occiput where the leather knot of the head *tefillin* is bound (also corresponding on the inside to the atlas vertebra), is where according to numerous Torah traditions, as Ramchal explained above, a human being is resurrected from the dead[47]. The Kotel may look "dead", but you cannot always tell what is on the "inside" of a wall from its outer covering.

One of the most powerful and direct techniques for entering into and stimulating the Foundation Stone, while simultaneously entering into and stimulating one's own Jerusalem of the Mind, is in the secret polarity that is found between these two terminals of the Wall and the Rock. This is the secret circuit embedded between a "wall and a hard place", between the Western Wall and the Hard Place of the Foundation Stone. For the one who understands, the millennial history of the pain and suffering, joys and victories embedded in the stones of the Kotel can be used, like a battering ram directed at the Foundation Stone, in order to "rock it", squeeze it and release its higher-dimensional global DMT. The Western Wall is only half of the story of the future redemption. The future, rapidly accelerating now in our generation, is being stimulated by the discovery and scientific speculation concerning the pineal gland, DMT and its role in consciousness and the divine realm. The higher-dimensional analog to human DMT—Adamic DMT— is the elixir of Jewish juice that supra-naturally binds *Klal Yisrael* together. It is the phenomenon of "Jewish DMT" that is the secret to the otherwise inexplicable unity and indestructibility of the Jewish Nation. The moral of the story? Don't only pray at the Wall, but also *squeeze the Rock*.

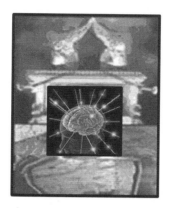

10. **Activating the Pineal/Peniel Circuit**

As explained above, the Peniel Principle is predicated upon the ancient Torah tradition that the two Foundation Stones are inextricably interconnected and literally share a common resonance, each one entrained within the other. The goal of Peniel consciousness is, in affect, to "rub" one "rock" against the other, just as if we were striking one rock against another in order to spark a fire. Together, the two centers — the micro-center and the macro- center — open up a pathway or circuit. This process is actually very simple and virtually guaranteed to work because these circuits are fundamentally already here, the "grooves" being hardwired into the planet. Just as in the human body neural pathways are already built into us, likewise the inter-dimensional circuits that spread out from Jerusalem throughout the world are built into creation. This is the esoteric meaning of the verse, "For out of Zion [another code name for the Foundation Stone] will go forth Torah [here referring to the renewed Torah consciousness of the Messianic Age].

The future waterways referred to above are not only something that will be created totally new. These virtual global "cerebrospinal neural networks" and passage ways already have their channels carved out in the extra-dimensional planes. The circuits or "tunnels" are already here and we only have to "get our motor running", and our pulsating thought waves will find their own way and level. The Talmudic Sage-Mystics also allude to these hidden meridians where they enigmatically inform us that, "In the future the level of *kedusha*/holiness of the Holy of Holies will spread throughout the entire Temple Mount, the *kedusha* of the Temple Mount will spread throughout all of Jerusalem, the *kedusha* of Jerusalem will spread throughout all of Eretz Yisrael and the *kedusha* of Eretz Yisrael will spread throughout the entire world". From the perspective of the higher-dimensional "future" this is already the case and this is especially true now in our generation, the "Final Generation" (the term used by the Talmudic Sage-Mystics), as we are poised on the cusp of the Davidic Messianic Age. If the light is more accessible now, then the pathways of those lights are also more accessible. In other words, there is a microcosmic fractal chip of the Foundation Stone potentially literally everywhere. We only have to uncover the "Jerusalem connection" wherever we are in space or in time and it becomes activated right then and there within our own consciousness, even affecting the space around us. The Liquid Light of Jerusalem is spreading out to encompass the entire world and it is here now to be utilized and applied.[48]

As mentioned, an important reason why the Peniel system works is because we are not creating anything new or trying to make something happen that may or may not occur in the future. As we are teetering on the edge of the Messianic Age, the Living Liquid is going to flow sooner or later. This is an immutable Torah fact as explicitly stated in the words of the prophets and amplified by the unbroken tradition of the Talmudic Sage-Mystics up until this day. The P2P question, however, is not when will the higher-dimensional Adamic "DMT" begin to flow. Rather, how can we help accelerate the inevitable now, sooner than later? It is important to realize that from the higher-dimensional perspective of the "future" messianic reality, this vortex is already emanating a stream of liquid consciousness. We are only creating a vessel or "docking station" for it to manifest now in our present state of reality.

With practice, this physical/spiritual circuitry becomes a self-perpetuating feedback loop with growing intention and intensity. The power that can be generated with a conscious pineal body by one individual is unlimited. The power generated by a small network of active like-minds with conscious pineal bodies is staggering. P2P is for real; it can be done and it must be done. Time is of the essence and the essence is to be found in our endogenous DMT and in its analog, the *Mayim Chayim*, the Living Liquid congealed, as it were, within the Foundation Stone. As the Talmudic Sage-Mystic Hillel is quoted, "If I am not for myself who will be for me? And if not now, when?

There are a number of very simple ways to do this. By experimenting, you find the one(s) that work for you. The P2P techniques are simple because they are essentially all done visually, kinesthetically and viscerally. You simply project your thought and "you are where your mind is", as is well known. The operational goal is to regularly get "inside" the Foundation Stone that is under the dome on the Temple Mount. Once inside, you "arouse" it with whatever you have at that moment. This can be prayer, petition, even directed anger at God as well as anger at all those who would humiliate us, torture us and annihilate us. (The role of Holocaust memories and imagery, like the diamond head of a drill bit, is an extremely powerful tool to help "break open" the Foundation Stone. The incomprehensible horror and inexpressible anger associated with the Holocaust is especially powerful when directed like a laser beam at and then through the Foundation Stone into the higher- dimension). The source of stimulation can be personal pain as well as collective pain, personal pleasure, cries of devastation and tears of ecstasy. You can consciously direct the pleasure while you are eating, while you are thinking and even while you are sleeping (if you program yourself as you fall asleep).

Various methods to "squeeze the rock" are mentioned directly or indirectly throughout this work. Regardless of what method one is using at any given time or place, there is one immutable axiom: Polarity. There are always two terminals — the Jerusalem pineal of each and everyone's Mind, and the Jerusalem Peniel — the Foundation Stone — of all humanity. This ratio recapitulates itself in the two terminals of the Wall and the Foundation Stone. Part II will supply the blueprints for the actual construction of the inner technology that will enable any serious practitioner to visit the City of Luz, the higher-dimensional Foundation Stone and the New Jerusalem.

Putting the P2P methodology into practice achieves numerous goals:

1. Everyone, Jew and non-Jew alike, can now become an active "soldier" in the army of the God of Israel. In the face of Israel's sworn enemies no one need feel helpless and impotent as to what he or she can do *right now* to help save Israel and the world as well as to wake up one's own consciousness.

2. We can defend ourselves against our Moslem enemies — the Children of Ishmael — with the power of the Foundation Stone's Living Liquid

and higher-dimensional "conquering love". From this perspective there is no need for outward destruction of the giant *klipah*/dome that has imprisoned our Foundation Stone. In order for Mashiach and the Messianic Era to arrive, we do not have to physically remove the Dome of the Rock. Rather, we can "liquefy" the Foundation Stone with the power of P2P consciousness. This will cause it to begin dripping its universal healing waters. This is true "mind over matter".

3.   We can help wake up the dormant Jews of the world (the vast majority of Jews today) by stimulating the very center of global Jewish consciousness. P2P, in computer language, also stands for "peer to peer". We can create a virtual internet (or more correctly, an *intra*net, a "private internet") of pineal nodes that send out frequencies from one pineal to another (*da'at* to *da'at*). This is serious Jerusalem computer power.

4.   Each one of us can begin to open up our *own* pineal gland and release our own "river of light" produced right within our own brain! This is a true Torah path to direct and experiential enlightenment, non-ordinary consciousness and directly "knowing" one's Creator.

5.   With P2P consciousness, every act and thought, regardless of when and where, can be infused with new meaning and mission. This is all the more so when the Peniel Principle is interfaced with prayer and/or meditation. All prayer, medita-

tion and contemplation are now also done with one's consciousness projected *into* the Foundation Stone underneath the dome at the apex of the Temple Mount.

There are numerous ways to stimulate the global pineal gland the Jerusalem Foundation Stone. This, in turn, radiates back to each one's personal pineal gland. Which method one works with will depend upon many factors, set and setting and the "tools" one uses will continue molding one's level of growth. Along with the methods described here, it is possible and even encouraged, for everyone to develop additional modes of P2P meditation and prayer strategy.

Fundamentally, the goal for a Jew (and Philo-Semites and Noahides alike) is to keep Jerusalem at the center of one's personal consciousness while simultaneously projecting one's self to the Jerusalem center of global consciousness. If you make Jerusalem the center of your consciousness (i.e., literally "squeeze" the Foundation Stone into your pineal gland), then Jerusalem with make you the center of her consciousness (i.e., you will be in the center of the Foundation Stone).

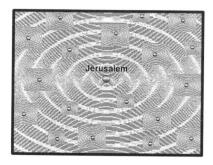

11. Iterating "Jerusalems of the Mind"

The question is asked—and must be asked—why does the Supreme Mind, the Holy One, the Source of all Blessings need us and our DMT-producing pineal glands to stimulate the redemption process and help Him usher in the Messianic Age? According to the hundreds of explicit and implicit descriptions in the Torah and by the Talmudic Sage-Mystics concerning the Foundation Stone, should it not have the power to redeem itself? If God is supremely omnipotent why does Heaven need our assistance? Truly, this question goes to the root of the profound enigmatic relationship between all things that are human and accessible and all things that are Godly and inaccessible. This cosmic puzzle has been probed and explored for millennia by the Talmudic Sage-Mystics as well as by theologians and philosophers the world over and is a large tome unto itself. Here, only a fraction of the answer to the difficulty, as it pertains to the Peniel Principle, is presented.

The Temple, with its precursor in the *Mishkan* (Tabernacle) did not operate on its own, even with the masses of Kohanim and Levites who orchestrated and performed all the necessary ritual functions within. The success—indeed the very existence of the *Mishkan* and its successor the Temple—depended upon the collective actions and consciousness of the people. This is evident from numerous verses in the Torah, one of the most explicit being,

"They shall make a Sanctuary for Me — so that I may dwell among them" (Exodus 25-8). The sages point out that the Holy One specifically does not say that I may dwell "in it" — the Sanctuary, but rather "among them", i.e., within their collective body, heart and soul — the consciousness of the people.

In other words, the Temple structure and all of its vessels and artifacts are wired only to work when the nation itself is working them. The Temple — and the Even Shetiya, which the entire edifice of the Temple is conceptually and literally resting upon — is dependent on our active participation. In and of itself, this should not surprise us as other Scriptural verses are equally clear that the upper realm is inextricably interdependent with the lower realm. The Torah declares, "Give strength to God" and "When I call upon the Name of HaShem give power to our God". The inverse is also true, "The Rock that begat you, you have weakened, i.e., our earthly actions, speech and thought can also affect the heavenly realms adversely. These formulas are in accord with the axiom which states, "Nothing descends from Above unless it is initially aroused from below". We are more than symbolic partners with the Divine we are inseparable and we affect each other.[49]

The apparent paradox that the Divine realm, also literally and not only metaphorically, is uniquely in need of our prayers and directed thoughts, brings us back to the riddle of the Heavenly Jerusalem, "The Holy One said, I will not enter the Celestial Jerusalem until I enter the earthly Jerusalem". As formulated above, the "Jerusalem from Below" is also referring to the Jerusalem with its Foundation Stone that resides *within* each and every one of us. As Jews we have the innate ability as individuals and as a collective to initially enter our own inner sanctum thus enabling the Divine to enter the Heavenly Jerusalem. The new and growing knowledge about the role of the pineal gland in human consciousness and the otherworldly nature of endogenous dimethyltryptamine is springing forth from the scientific and medical communities. Without this occurring, we would not have the necessary model to begin to glimpse the staggering profundity of the prophetic Living Liquid. This inter-dimensional substance is literally on the threshold ready to flood the world with messianic consciousness. It needs our assistance to reveal itself now in the world and we more than need its assistance. As the motto goes, "If we work it, it will work and if we don't then it won't".

In the section above, The Messianic Role of the Pineal Gland, it was explained that DMT, an enigmatic liquid molecular transmitter, has been found to exist throughout the human bloodstream and within every cell of the body. A hypothesis, based upon strong circumstantial evidence, is that the equally enigmatic pineal organ is capable, under specific conditions, of producing relatively large amounts of DMT, which is then immediately released into the "waterways" of the body — the cerebrospinal fluid. The infusion into the brain of this "spirit molecule" has extraordinary and, as of yet, inexplicable effects upon human consciousness and our very concept of what reality even is.

The fact, however, that every separate cell also manufactures DMT implies that the pineal is a massive "mother ship" to billions of smaller satellite ships. Each cell has its own individual "consciousness" and is a center onto itself (and depending upon which bodily tissue or organ it is found within, it will have additional unique qualities, e.g., a foot cell versus a heart or brain cell). Truly, from a holistic point of view, they all work together and need each other yet the whole being greater than the sum of the individual parts. The pineal, located centrally in the brain, appears to be the meta-center of all the DMT-producing cells — a virtual "mother ship" of collective DMT cell consciousness. Moreover, all the billions of cells together cannot even come near to producing the amount of DMT that the mother pineal is capable of producing and the effects she has upon the entire body *and* soul of a person.

From the Torah perspective of the Talmudic Sage-Mystics, this model reveals a crucial spiritual truth regarding the ancient legacy of the global role and mission of Jerusalem and her Foundation Stone. Once again, the axiom "From my body I will envision God" (Job) equates the global body to the human body. As the pineal body—the personal Foundation Stone of consciousness—is to every cell in the human body, so is the geographical, spiritual history and location of Jerusalem's Foundation Stone to the world and all humanity. The Torah not only maintains that there are numerous holy places, sacred vortices and energy centers located all around the globe, but *all* the sacred "stones" (e.g., Stonehenge), "rocks" (e.g., the various pyramids) and cities (e.g., Machu Picchu) are rooted and emanating *out* of Jerusalem! Moreover, just as a pineal gland is useless without the rest of the body, Jerusalem cannot be complete without every single one of these geographical and historical locations reuniting with her.

The Peniel Principle, utilizing the pineal model, now enables us to understand a number of formula-statements of the Talmud—not to mention the hundreds of Scriptural verses—concerning the future, higher-dimensional state of Jerusalem with the Foundation Stone at its core. "Jerusalem will become a lighthouse [of consciousness] unto the nations", "Jerusalem will become a metropolis [of consciousness] to the world" and "The holiness of Jerusalem [consciousness] will spread out to encompass the entire world".[50] These are not, according to the unbroken tradition of the Talmudic Sage-Mystics, mythological or ethnocentric platitudes. Rather, if we now understand the Foundation Stone and Jerusalem as the "pineal" and "brain" of the world, they are literally true. When the pineal/Foundation Stone of a person is (theoretically) fully activated, then relative to the entirety of the person, an amazing phenomenon is realized. It is a "lighthouse" of consciousness unto the other "nation-parts of the body", it is a "metropolis" of consciousness to the organ-parts of the body and its holiness literally spreads out to encompass all the energy vortices within the body of the entire person.

The formulation is clear and simple. If there is a center to our consciousness (the pineal) and all humanity is one Adamic mind and body, then there must also be a center to world consciousness. As the pineal body is the best candidate for a true meta-center of human consciousness, there is no better candidate for global consciousness than the ancient city of Jerusalem and the cosmic Foundation Stone at its center. With even a small network of global iterating "Jerusalems of the Mind", we truly fulfill and activate the *mitzvah* and *tikun* of "praying for the peace of Jerusalem.

12. A Torah Lesson from "Horton Hears a Who!"

At the inception of the Messianic Age the prophets clearly tell us that there will be, "… liquid coming out from under the threshold" at the entrance to the Holy of Holies. The question, however, persists: Isn't a Foundation Stone campaign to "squeeze the rock" magical thinking at best or worse — religious dogma for the faithful few? Can the prophetic torrential river of Living Liquid be stimulated to begin trickling even *before* its time — whether it is years or even just minutes before its "due date"? Moreover, can the power of just one individual alone or even the power of numerous networking groups, have the ability to be *that one* to stimulate the Foundation Stone and push it over its threshold?

There are many deep Torah-based explanations for this phenomenon as to why it can and even *must* be so. The most simple explanation, however, as to why this is true is impressively made from a children's story that many of us grew up with (which more recently was made into a movie). Dr. Seuss' Horton Hears a Who! delivers the message that the final trigger, the simple switching on of the light, can indeed be in the hands of even one person, let alone multitudes, regardless of whether they are Jewish or not, men or women and, as in the case of Horton's story, even in the hands of a child!

Horton is a friendly elephant who one day has a strange encounter. A dust speck floats past him in the air and he hears a tiny yelp coming from it. Believing that an entire family of microscopic creatures is living on that speck, he places it on top of a pink clover that he holds in his trunk. Horton finds out the speck harbors the city of Who-ville and all its inhabitants. The other animals of the jungle, however, refuse to believe Horton. Moreover, they are determined to destroy the flower to make their point that Horton is making up the story. The population of Who-ville is in a mad panic to save their world from complete annihilation. The mayor enlists all of his people to make noise by shouting, "We are here!" as well as playing a variety of instruments and making every noise conceivable, so the disbelieving animals can hear them. Alas, although every single person, young and old, is making noise and yelling, nothing can be heard from the flower. Doom is imminent. At the last minute, however, a young teenage boy runs up the highest tower and yells, "Yop!" Just before the microscopic world is to be destroyed, that one little sound *combined* with the cacophony of noise from the entire city causes their collective noise to be heard by the other animals. One single person — and a child at that — was what caused the entire population to hit critical mass saving an entire world from annihilation.

The Torah lesson from Horton Hears a Who is obvious. It doesn't matter whether one is a Jew or a gentile, a man or a woman, a Torah scholar or an uneducated seeker, a *tzadik*/saint or just one of the common folk. We can all be part of the cosmic game plan and accelerate the stimulation of the Foundation Stone using the power of the Peniel Principle to stimulate the trigger to hit critical mass. Ultimately, it is simply a matter of striking two stones against each other—the Wall and the Rock—to produce just a little spark. One little spark, however, under the right conditions can go a long way. And the right conditions are right now.[51] Then, "The stone which the builders have rejected has become the Head Stone". (Psalm 118:21-23).[52]

> *The Peniel Principle is the royal road to Torah Consciousness*
> *and the pilgrim's path to the Foundation Stone*
> *of Jerusalem of the Mind.*

"He gives wisdom to those who have wisdom". (Book of Daniel)

"The one who understands will understand" (Talmudic Sage-Mystics)

13. Additional Section for Noahides
(Righteous Gentiles)
King David, Araunah the Jebusite
and the Secret behind the Foundation Stone

Noahides, Evangelical Christians, "Ephramites", "Ten Tribers", Bible-based gentiles and any non-Jewish supporters of Israel are constantly struck by the painful phenomenon of assimilated Jews, left-leaning "rabbis" and secularized Israelis who are working against God's Torah and His Will as mandated in the Torah. How is it possible for a gentile to love and support Jews, Judaism and the Land of Judah more than a Jew? The prophesies for millions of Jews returning to their God-given home in the Biblical Land of Israel and other explicit signs being so obvious, why do lovers of Israel and Philo-Semites "get it", while the majority of Jews throughout the world today are quite literately "in the dark"? (Tragically, there are even Jews who actively work against the Creator's plan for the unique mission of His unique people in His unique Holy Land). Why doesn't the collective soul of the Jewish people see the very treasures they are sitting upon, its cosmic mission to restore all humanity to a single consciousness, and not hear the living legacy of an almost 4,000 year old tradition of Torah with its instructions?

Additionally, there is a crisis that confronts all of us who are

Torah and Bible-based that is literally a matter of life and death for the Nation of Israel, if not for much of the world. This dilemma appears intractable and, from a Biblical Torah perspective, it is intractable because there is no human solution in God's cosmic End Times. This is the rise of Islam, the ever-increasing menace of the descendants of Ishmael. It is their obsessive intent to "reclaim" the Holy Land — and specifically the Temple Mount — as a part of their former Islamic empire, as well as parts of Europe, if not the entire world. This necessitates the obliteration of Israel and the subjugation everywhere of Jews, Noahides and Christians to their dictates — if not to forced conversion under the sword. The question is, aside from praying and crying out for the Messiah to rectify this impossible situation, what can anyone do in a real, practical and "hands on" manner to defend ourselves and to defeat our enemies? Certainly doing more *mitzvot*, good deeds and praying more consciously must continue, but the brutal truth is, as we can plainly see in the world, these methods are not affecting the paradigm shift in world consciousness that was needed *yesterday*. Must we remain feeling impotent and without real recourse?

Noahide consciousness — multitudes of gentiles waking up to Biblical truth and to the God of Israel — is blossoming worldwide. This grass-roots movement, in all of its various forms continues, almost miraculously, its accelerating growth. Correspondingly, there are now appearing in our generation, revelations coming to light about the role such conscious gentiles can and must play to assist the Jewish Nation in the final hours of God's cosmic drama. Many Noahides, their religious colleagues and acquaintances feel a sense of frustration and impatience as to their role *right now* to help the people and Land of Israel. For some, sitting on the sidelines and rooting for Israel, although meritorious and righteous in its own right, is not enough. Their hearts are aflame for the God of Israel and the desire to be inducted into the frontlines of battle.

However, neither the general Jewish community from without nor the specialized Torah community from within has yet to supply a coherent and detailed plan for the necessary pro-Israel "special ops" being called for.

The answer, however, to both of the questions asked above is profoundly simple but unexpected. The soul of the Jewish people simply needs someone to switch on the light in the collective mind of Israel so that the descendants of Jacob can begin to see clearly the depth of their own consciousness. Jews who are currently unconscious will then, by divine design, naturally understand who they are in God's cosmic drama. They will then intuitively know what they must now do in our period of the Final Redemption, especially in regard to the ever-growing enemies of Israel and Jews worldwide. As explained above, the mission of the Jewish Nation has everything it needs to take off and to fulfill its destined mission; all the supplies are onboard and all systems are "go". Most Jews in the world today, however, simply can't see the control panel of their own ship because someone simply needs to turn on the light for them. Although our sworn enemies are fast upon us and the spiritual geopolitical clock is forebodingly past the eleventh hour, there is still time to turn the lights on in the collective Jewish mind so it can awaken and be activated. Here is where select non-Jews, securely attached to the God of Israel and to the collective Jewish consciousness can — and perhaps must — play a pivotal role.

Yet, in order for such gentiles to play a pivotal role, a crucial question (for both Torah-based Jews and Bible-based gentiles alike) must be asked. Why would the Creator orchestrate the End Times in such a way that the final trigger leading to Jewish *tikun* and global redemption also resides in the hands of non-Jews, even if they be the most righteous among the Seventy Nations — (e.g., the quintessential *ger toshav*)? Initially, from both a conventional

Torah perspective and from a simple Noahide perspective, this appears strange and even ludicrous — if not heretical. How is it possible that the salvation of humanity can also depend upon a non-Jewish source turning on the light of consciousness for the Jews to see the mission of their own collective soul? Are not even the best of the righteous of the Seventy Nations only stationed on the periphery of the Nation of Israel to "protect and to reflect", i.e., to act as a wall of protection against the enemies of Israel and to act as a mirror reflecting back support, blessings and praise? This function may be true for the majority of God's army of Torah-based gentiles, but it appears that this is not the case for all Noahides — not those who hear a call to inner arms.

There are a number of reasons, of which only a few are being presented here, for the astounding ability of select gentiles to come to the aid of Jewish consciousness. One surprising reason is this: The Foundation Stone, before it became the location of the Holy of Holies, was originally a threshing floor owed by a non-Jew from whom King David purchased it. Here is where David's son Solomon would build the first Temple of Jerusalem. As told in the Book of II Samuel, this was Araunah the Jebusite. The rabbinic tradition (BT *Avodah Zara* 24b) tells us that this non-Jew was, in fact, a God fearing and God-loving Noahide observing the Seven Universal Noahide Laws[53]. Moreover, he had converted and was received by King David to be a *ger toshav*, a resident convert and honored Noahide living among Torah observant Jews!

There is, however, more to this gentile owner of a threshing floor than meets the eye. In what appears to be an obvious incongruency in Scripture, Araunah the Jebusite has two names. At the end of the Book of Samuel where he is first mentioned he is called Araunah (or Aravnah in Modern Hebrew). Yet, in Chronicles (I Chapter 21:15), the final book of the Tanach, he is referred to only as "Ornan". Now, if his name is Ornan, why was he originally called Araunah? The Talmudic Sage-Mystics reveal to us that Scripture intentionally altered his name (as in a myriad of other similar cases with proper nouns throughout the Tanach) to reveal an important secret about the inner nature of Araunah and the spiritual essence of his threshing floor where David and Solomon would build the Temple.

The bedrock that was being used as a threshing floor was the very primeval Foundation Stone (as explained above) upon which would soon rest the *Aron HaBrit* — the Ark of the Covenant. The Hebrew word that spells Araunah can also be read, by changing only one vowel sound, as *Aronah*. *Aron*, meaning ark, is in the masculine gender whereas *aronah* would also mean ark only that it would be in the feminine gender (all nouns in Hebrew are either male or female, there being no neuter form). That is, *aronah*/ark is spelled with the added letter *"hey"* on the end making it grammatically the feminine gender form of the corresponding masculine form of *aron*/ ark. (Neither of these should be confused with the personal name *Aharon*/Aaron that is from a different root.)

Now, why two aspects of an ark? The *aronah*/ark, as stated in the Zohar and further explained by its commentaries, represents the "backside" to the face of the holy *aron*/ark. This is based upon the well-known principle of polarity that "One thing parallels another" (Ecclesiastes 7:14). The recounting of the episode in Chronicles is kabbalisticaly qualifying the original event as recorded in Samuel to inform us that King David is extracting and elevating the status of the Foundation Stone from its lower dimension of *aronah*/ark and its spiritual imprisonment to the higher dimension of the holy *aron*/ ark. This is in conformity with the also well-known formula that "The *klipah*/shell always precedes the fruit."

It is important to understand that the sages are not implying that Araunah was the evil *klipah* (the constricting shells holding the purpose and function of the Foundation Stone in spiritual captivity). Rather, as well known, there are four major layers or membranes that cover, constrict and hold the sparks of holiness in captivity. The fourth membrane, which is called *nogah*/glow, can oscillate between serving the "other side" of the three negative shells or serving the "holy side." When something is in a *nogah*/glowing state then it, like fruit that has just ripened, can be retrieved, redeemed and reabsorbed back into the holy. Araunah, as a conscious Noahide and intrinsically interconnected with the family of Israel, has evolved out of the "thick" and impenetrable *klipot*/shells of the Canaanite nations and has entered into the increasingly holy and refined state of *nogah*. The Foundation Stone, as well as the adjacent property where the future Temple would be built, has followed the same course. King David is now consciously and methodically elevating the "backside" of the *aronah*/ark to prepare for the permanent home of the sacred *aron*/ark that has come to spiritual fruition.

The essence of Araunah, functioning as a transitional phase in the process towards the final *tikun*/rectification of the collapse of Adam and his higher-dimensional reality, also explains another apparent incongruency in the text. When first introduced, he is simply Araunah the Jebusite and that is how he has been known for millennia. In a following verse (24:23), however, he is referred to as King Araunah. Now, was he or wasn't he? [54] In truth, he was only a chieftain or prince of his clan and not an actual king. Rather, it was only *after* he offered and was willing to relinquish ownership of the Foundation Stone to David does the verse refer to him as a "king", i.e., a "king" over his strategic role in the "*nogahite*" transition of his threshing floor into the Foundation Stone. The Foundation Stone on Mt. Moriah was originally "midwifed" into this world through a righteous Noahide who had, in effect, been guarding and protecting it until the King of the Jews was ready to put it into action. Araunah, in his role as *Aronah*, was a true king of the emerging luminous glow of Noahide conscious-ness.[55]

Presently, with the Foundation Stone on the threshold of its final rebirth, it may be that once again a Noahide — this time pos-sibly in the form of a network of Noahides — will play a critical role in Israel's redemption process. It is also relevant to know that the Foundation Stone was then being used specifically as a "threshing floor" by the Jebusites alluding to the fundamental role the Noahide may need to play in the final redemption process. The earlier process of "threshing grain" is a corollary to the neces-sary process now of striking the rock in order to awaken it from its dormant state. A Noahide enabled the Foundation Stone to as-cend from its surrounding *klipah* of the Canaanite nations. Perhaps now it will be the Noahides who will once again play a pivotal role in the transitional process of removing the Foundation Stone from under its present *klipah* of Ishmael — *kipat haSelah* — the Dome of the Rock.

The transformation and redemption of the Foundation Stone began with a Noahide and it is fitting that its end should also in-volve Noahides. "The end result is rooted in the initial action" is a formulation that is well known among the Jewish sages. Who will step up to the plate? Who desires to be directly involved in turn-ing on the light in the collective mind of the Nation of Israel and thus enabling them to defeat the enemy, win the final battles and bring the entire world to messianic consciousness? If you hear the calling to inner arms and you want to be that one or part of a net-work to turn on the light of Jewish consciousness, you can become an intrinsic part of the redemption process — the Jerusalem of the Mind and the secret of the Foundation Stone.

Endnotes

Part I

1 Talmud Tractate *Ta'anit* 5a. The quote in our editions of the Talmud actually states, "The Holy One, blessed be He said, 'I will not enter the celestial Jerusalem until I enter the earthly Jerusalem'". The phrase, however, used elsewhere in the Zohar and Midrash is, "The Holy one vowed…" and this is the how the statement is often quoted in rabbinic literature. (Another variation is, "He vowed that His *Shechinah* would not enter…". Midrash Tanchuma *Pekudei*). The Talmud here continues by asking rhetorically, "Is there then a celestial Jerusalem? Yes, as it is written (Psalms 122:3), 'The built-up Jerusalem will be like the city which is joined together with it'". The verse implies the existence of another city, which is a counterpart of the earthly Jerusalem (Rashi, *Ta'anit* 5a, See also, Zohar III 15b, II 131a, III 262b). The two Jerusalems and the two corresponding Temples are foundational in an authentic Torah cosmology. The Talmudic Sage-Mystics also refer to the two as the Jerusalem of *Olam Hazeh* (This World) and the Jerusalem of *Olam HaBah* (the Coming World, i.e., the higher-dimension. See e.g., Talmud *Bava Batra*, 75b.) One Hebrew index to statements of the sages lists over 200 separate and distinct references to "Jerusalem" with the majority explicitly or implicitly defining the higher- dimensional coordinates of the New Jerusalem of the future. Additionally, the Zohar has over 20 references to the "twin Jerusalems". Noteworthy, among many of the formulas revealing its inner nature is that, "Jerusalem has seventy names" (*Midrash Zuta*, Song of Songs, 1).

2 By the using the term *Talmudic Sage-Mystics*, I am including every patriarch, prophet, elder, Talmudic Sage, Jewish mystic and rabbi who form an unbroken tradition going back, not just to Moses upon Mt Sinai, but also back to the Patriarchs, Noah, Enoch and even to Adam. There was a living Talmudic tradition from the time of the Academy of Shem and Ever (Noah's son Shem and Shem's grandson Ever) long before it was written down beginning in the

2nd century C.E. The full term for this legacy is actually Talmudic *Science*-Sage-Mystic as every sage was also a master of the Seven Sciences (the various fields of secular natural sciences in each generation) together with having been initiated into the esoteric depths of the inner Torah — the Kabbalah. Following the canonization of the Talmud, however, the vast interdisciplinary nature of the traditional Torah polymath began to erode and give way to specialization and, in some Torah circles, crucial aspects of the true Kabbalah were lost. Over the last millennia, the original legacy, however, continued to be maintained by many hundreds of elite Torah masters. In the last 250 years, the personality who was the quintessential Talmudic Scientist-Sage-Mystic was the Gaon of Vilna with his unique cadre of disciples from the town of Shklov. (For a full account of the history and personality of the Talmudic Sage-Mystic, see my two-volume work, *The Secret Doctrine of the Gaon of Vilna* as well as Step Four in my *Beyond Kabbalah — The Teachings That Cannot Be Taught*).

3   *Mishnah Middot, Ma'aseh HaKorbanot* 2:14, *Melachim* 11:1

4   Rashi, *Sukkah* 41a, *Rosh HaShanah* 30a. The Talmudic school of Tosofot (14th century) also supports this view in *Sukkah* 41a and *Shavuot* 15b. Although Rashi and Tosofot do not quote a source for the descent of a divinely constructed Temple, the Tosofot in *Shavuot* 15b does reference a Midrash as a source (the location of that Midrash is apparently no longer known).

5   This is the main finding of a poll commissioned by the Knesset Television Channel and carried out by the Panel Institute: 49% said they want the rebuilding of the Holy Temple, while 23% said they do not. The remainder said they were unsure. The public is about evenly split on whether they believe the rebuilding will happen, with a slight edge — 42% to 39% — to those who believe the Third Holy Temple will be rebuilt. Should the State of Israel take active steps towards the reconstruction? 48% said no, while 27% said yes. (IsraelNationalNews.com)

6   A mere visit to the holy site in the year 2,000 by then-Opposition Leader Ariel Sharon is blamed by Arabs for having sparked the Oslo War, a terrorist onslaught that claimed nearly 1,000 Israeli lives in just over four years — (although as known, the uprising was planned by leading Palestinian

Authority figures for months beforehand).

7   A corollary view is that we are also not permitted to attempt to accelerate the redemption process but that it will come in its time, which only God knows. There are many, however, in the tradition of the Talmudic Sage-Mystics none the least among them the Gaon of Vilna and his disciples of Shklov that staunchly maintain that it is God's will that we must be proactive in stimulating the redemption. I have detailed this doctrine in my two volume work *The Secret Doctrine of the Gaon of Vilna.*

8   What was forbidden to investigate and expound upon just yesterday becomes permissible today. This is felt by every true exegete. Numerous matters whose awesome nature repelled one from even approaching in previous generations, behold, they are easily grasped today. This is because the gates of human understanding below have been opened up as a result of the steadily increasing flow of Divine revelations above". R. Shlomo Eliyashiv, *Leshem Sh'vo V'Achlamah, Chelek HaBi'urim*, p. 21d.

9   This same tradition has been handed down by an unexpected yet highly authoritative source, R. Yisrael Salanter (1810-1883), the leader of the Mussar Movement. In confirmation of the statement of the Zohar, he is said to have commented, "Prior to 1840 the study of Kabbalah was a closed book to all but the initiated." The Kabbalist, R. Shlomo Eliyashiv, who quotes this tradition, continues, "Thus, from 1840 onwards, permission has been granted for those who truly desire to enter within. The Kabbalah is no longer the private domain of the initiated masters." *Leshem Sh'vo VeAchlamah, Sefer De'ah* 1:5:4 (p. 76).

10   The underlying axiom behind the relationship between the scientific vessels and the lights of Torah is replicating (i.e., fractal iteration) exactly that of the eternal dynamic between HuG — the *hasadim* and *gevurot* — the divine masculine and feminine forces within the *Ohr Ain Sof.* For a detailed analysis of this phenomenon and more of its applications see the chapter on HuG in *Beyond Kabbalah.* For more amplification of the intrinsic divine roots of the Seven Natural Sciences that emanate out of the Torah (which in turn emanates out of the Supernal Torah, the "Mind of God"), see my *Secret Doctrine of the Gaon of Vilna,* Volume II, Chapter 3, especially Fractal 4 (p. 127).

There the Gaon is quoted as saying, "The distillations [i.e., iterations] of Torah are the natural sciences of the lower world".

11 For the one who understands, the foreign dome surrounding the Foundation Stone is a type of giant *o'rlah* (foreskin) covering, constricting and holding the Foundation Stone imprisoned and preventing it from performing its true spiritual function. At its core this phenomenon is, as known in esoteric Judaism, fractally iterating the deeper truth and purpose behind the ritually mandated Jewish rite of circumcision. For further explanation of the secret behind circumcision, see my *Secret Doctrine of the Gaon of Vilna*, Volume II, Chapter 3, Leviathan. (Interestingly, *Kipat HaSelah* — the Dome of the Rock as it is called in Hebrew — phonetically resonates with *k'lipat HaSelah* — meaning the covering, shell or *o'rlah* of the Rock!)

12 Tractate *Yoma* 54b.

13 Zohar *VaYechi* 1:231.

14 "It appears to me that this [primeval] point is what the sages refer to as the "Foundation Stone" from which the world was woven". (Nachmanides, Commentary on Genesis on the verse, "And God said..."). "Nachmanides wrote that this [Foundation Stone] is the secret of the primeval matter which the Greeks call "*hyly*", the archetypal substance that is able to receive form. From it the entire world was formulated." (*Kehilot Ya'akov*, entry *"Ab"*)

15 Obviously, it is not the molecular material of the rock itself that is sacred but rather the rock is a vortex for an inter-dimensional nexus point that is "anchored" into our dimension specifically at this spatial coordinate. Consequently, the rock, in this case, is imbued with *kedusha*/holiness. Likewise, as we direct our thoughts and prayers to the Foundation Stone (see further below and in Part II) it is only acting as the "circuit" or "wires" though which the Divine and human "electricity" are flowing to and fro. Accordingly, we are praying through the Foundation Stone to the Holy One, Blessed be He, and not to the Foundation Stone. This principle applies to all sacred locations, structures and artifacts in the Torah tradition.

16 In order to create a finite universe the Ohr (Infinite Light) of the Ain Sof undergoes a process of contraction known as *tzimtzum*. Similarly, all forms

in creation — physical and spiritual — emerge from the Foundation Stone through iterations of the original *tzimtzum*. Each of these *tzimtzumim* is recorded in the Foundation Stone.

Rabbi Nachman of Breslov teaches (*Likutey Moharan* 61:6) "The Torah is like the tablets of stone (Ex. 24), which receives its illumination from the aspect of the Foundation Stone, for each thing in the world has a different quantity and quality of *tzimtzum*, and all the *tzimtzumim* in the world, all of them are inscribed in the Foundation Stone, from which the world was drawn forth, and they all receive from it, and there all the *tzimtzumim* are sweetened, for it is like the Upper Wisdom, like the Holy of Holies. For the intellect is called The Holy (see Zohar *Acharei* 61)… And also in general, to sweeten all the constrictions that may be from some *tzimtzum*, is impossible except by the aspect of the Upper Intellect, like the Holy of Holies, like the Foundation Stone as (see Zohar *Vayechi* p. 231 and Midrash Tanchuma, *Eikev*).

Additionally, he teaches that "The Tzadik of the Generation, who is like the Holy of Holies, like the Foundation Stone… and through [the tzadikim of the generation] all the judgments are sweetened, through the aspect of the Foundation Stone as mentioned above. And this is like the stones [souls] of Jacob, where all of them merged into the Foundation Stone". (*Likutey Moharan* 61:7)

17 Midrash Tanchuma *Kedoshim* Ch.10.

18 *Itinerarium Sacrae Scipturae*, Heinrich Bunting, 1545-1606.

19 The actual terminology in the Midrash reads, "…and the *Even Shetiyah* is [situated] in front of the *aron*". The Ark of the Covenant cannot literally be in the center of the Foundation Stone because it does not rest on the Foundation Stone, but rather it was placed just to the west and next to it.

20 There need not be any confusion here with the biblical event of Moses "hitting the rock" instead of speaking to it, as he had been directed to do so by God. Firstly, even if we were to describe the inner mechanism behind the methodology of Jerusalem of the Mind as "hitting" the Foundation Stone, it is only metaphorical. Obviously, we are not physically hitting the Founda-

tion Stone but only "hitting" it with our directed words through the intense emotions of our heart and the thoughts of our mind. Moses, however, actually hit the rock. Secondly, the event of hitting the rock occurred near the end of the Israelite's 40- year sojourn in the desert. At the beginning of the 40-year period, there was a similar event in which Moses was, in fact, directed by God to actually hit a rock, out of which a spring of water appeared. Here, his act of hitting the rock was a sanctification of God's Name and a necessary component effecting cosmic tikun. In other words, sometimes it is appropriate to hit and sometimes to speak. In any event, the method used here in Jerusalem of the Mind is fundamentally about "squeezing" or simply "massaging" the Foundation Stone in order to arouse it and help awaken it from its dormant state.

21   There is disagreement regarding the location of the "crown chakra". This is expected, as the various Oriental systems, from where the chakra system originates, are not monolithic in their traditions, if not also in their actual physiological description of brain and body anatomy. Moreover, there is the question as to whether or not the etheric realm of the chakras even needs to conform to a specific localized coordinate in our physical world. Additionally, the Eastern "crown chakra" and/or the Western anatomical pineal has popularly been identified with the sefiratic emanation known in esoteric Judaism as *keter*/crown. However, this coordinate in the higher-dimensional "Godhead", as known, has various modes and associated locations. Likewise, the anatomically lower *da'at*/middle brain also has various modes that functions in the capacity of *keter*. *Keter*, as with all the elements and processes in advanced Kabbalah, are relative to each other (A sliding scale of "absolute relativity"). Any given *keter*, for example, can also function as a *malchut*/kingdom — its apparent opposite. Therefore, the specific analogical association of the pineal gland with the "crown chakra" and the sefirah of *keter* require further investigation.

22   According to numerous reports, the consensus is that the naturally produced DMT, as well as in its synthetic form, is even more potent than the synthetically produced lysergic acid diethylamide — LSD. Consequently, in comparison

to LSD, psilocybin, mescaline, cannabis and other psychedelics (lit. "mind-manifesting") or entheogens (lit. "generating the divine"), DMT appears to occupy its own unique category of mind-altering substances. Apparently, DMT is not so much "altering" one's consciousness as it is altering one's dimension, i.e., it is capable of unveiling and transporting one into what appears to be parallel, freestanding realities that are as true and real as our commonly accepted world. For those familiar with the *partzufim*, from a Kabbalistic perspective I suggest that whereas the other substances, natural or synthetic, are rooted in *Imma*, the Divine Mother, DMT is rooted in *Abba*, the Divine Father. (The Divine Mother is well known to be the source of ecstatic wine intoxication when used for sacred purposes).

23   Rick Strassman, MD investigated the effects of N,N-dimethyltryptamine (DMT) while conducting research in the 1990s. During the project's five years, he administered approximately 400 doses of DMT to over 60 human volunteers. This research took place at the University of New Mexico's School of Medicine in Albuquerque, New Mexico where he was then tenured Associate Professor of Psychiatry. DMT is found naturally in various natural sources, and is related to human neurotransmitters such as serotonin and melatonin. DMT is naturally produced in small amounts in the brain and other tissues of humans and other mammals. Strassman hypothesizes that DMT is produced by the human brain in the pineal gland. He refers to DMT as the "spirit molecule". He has conjectured that when a person is approaching death, the pineal gland releases DMT, accounting for much of the imagery reported by survivors of near-death experiences (this is in addition to other phenomena related to the pineal gland). It is known from the field of embryology that DMT is released on the forty-ninth day of fetus development, something Dr. Strassman has attributed to being the beginning of the soul. [This generally conforms with the frequently quoted tradition in the Talmud that the human embryo does not actually begin to "form" into a complete being until the fortieth day of gestation, i.e., the soul has not yet incarnated into the embryo until the fortieth day.]

Further, Strassman has speculated that DMT is specifically manufactured in the pineal gland, largely because the necessary constituents needed to make

DMT are found in the pineal gland in substantially greater concentrations than any other part of the body. Several speculative, but not yet tested, hypotheses suggest that endogenous DMT, produced in the human brain, is involved in certain psychological and neurological states. It may play a role in mediating the visual effects of natural dreaming, and also near-death experiences, religious visions and other mystical states. He wrote about the research program in his book DMT: The Spirit Molecule, and a documentary movie several years in the making based, in part, on his book is now available to the public (*The Spirit Molecule* Nov. 2010).

24 The "image of God" is also known as *Adam Elyon* — "Supernal Man". The "image" is referring to a higher dimensional template, which cannot be visualized or even easily conceptualized because we are creatures bound by the constrictions of our three dimensional "Flatland". Yet, by analogical thinking we can perceive in ratio the relationship between the Divine and the human. For a full discussion of dimensionality, see my *Beyond Kabbalah*.

25 Ramchal, *Mishkeney Elyon,* last page, p.195. (An English translation is available under the title, *Secrets of the Future Temple* by Avraham Greenberg, The Temple Institute, 1999). Elsewhere, the Ramchal writes (*Razin Genizin* p. 30), "These 'waters' that will flow from the Holy of Holies, their source is from the 'Concealed Wisdom' (*Chochmah Steema'ah*, a coordinate in the Godhead, as known in the Zohar and throughout Lurianic Kabbalah). Similarly emphasizing the higher- dimensional nature of this substance, Ramchal's disciple and colleague R' Moshe David Valli writes (Commentary to Zechariah 14:8), "The Living Liquid (*Mayim Chayim*) is in the secret of the upper *chesed* [expanding Divinity] that goes forth from the Supernals from the Source of Life".

26 This fact, however, does not negate the possibility that this spiritual substance will also contain the element of water or its essences.

27 More specifically, the material substance of the Living Liquid is only the "outer garment" for the higher-dimensional consciousness carried within it. The two components, however, are interdependent and the question, until the Messianic Era is fully upon us, is for now moot.

28 Lit., "And it will be after this". The actual final messianic period (of Mashiach ben

David) is referred to as the "End of Days". According to some commentaries, however, the phrase, "It will be after this" always refers to a period of time *prior* to the final messianic redemption. Additionally, it is significant to note that the following verse (3-2) in Joel continues with, "Also upon the servants and maidservants in those days I will pour out My *ruach*/spirit".Even the gentiles, who will be interfacing with the Nation of Israel in synergistic union, will also be recipients of altered consciousness and messianic light. This is cosmically logical as in the higher-dimensional non-local space-time fabric of the Messianic Era and beyond there will fundamentally be only one Adamic consciousness and a singular Adamic reality. The current distinctions between Jew and righteous non-Jew (Noahide), although eternal in their essence, will no longer be bound by our current laws of hierarchical distinction, but rather reality will be of a *holoarchical* nature (i.e., holographically hierarchical). (It has been suggested, in the context developed below concerning the secret of the Kotel/Western Wall, that the righteous of the nations must grab hold not only to the "hem of the garment" (i.e., the *tzitzit*/tassels mentioned in Zechariah) of the Jews, but also to the "coat-tails" (i.e., *Kotel*) of the Nation of Israel). The Midrash (Ecclesiastes Rabba 90:2-1) also uses this verse from the Book of Joel as a proof-text to indicate that this was, in fact, the case in the time of King Solomon (conceptually, if not also literally), i.e. that almost 3,000 years ago during the reign of Solomon righteous gentiles were also the recipients of *ruach haKodesh*.

29   This specific event, on the simple level, did not take place at the same earthly location of Jacob's dream on Mount Moriah. However, as is known in the Kabbalah, the terms *Peniel* (Face of God), *Ohrpeniel* (Light of the Face of God), *Sar haPanim* (Prince of the Face, i.e., Metatron) are all aspects or iterations of the same spiritual phenomenon, i.e., the primordial Divine Light. This is also a deeper significance of *Birkat Kohanim* — the Priestly Blessing. "May HaShem cause His *face* (*panim*) to shine upon you and be gracious unto you".

One of the other code names for Peniel is Luz, which explicitly is another name for Jerusalem. There are three texts that refer to Luz.

1.   "Jacob left Beersheba and headed toward Charan. He came

to a familiar place and spent the night there because the sun had already set. Taking some stones, he placed them at his head and lay down to sleep there. He had a vision in a dream. A ladder was standing on the ground, and its top reached up toward heaven. God's angels were going up and down on it. Suddenly he saw God standing over him... Jacob awoke from his sleep. 'God is truly in this place,' he said, 'It must be God's temple. It is the gate to heaven!' Jacob got up early in the morning and took the stone that he had placed under his head. He stood it up as a pillar and poured oil on top of it. He named the place God's Temple (Beth El). The town's original name, however, had been Luz". (Genesis 28-10,22)

2. "Jacob and all the people with him came to Luz (*Luza*) in the land of Canaan — that is, to Beit El. He built an altar there, and he named the place El Beit El (Beit El's God) since this was the place where God was revealed to him when he was fleeing from his brother". (Genesis 35-6)

3. "The house of Joseph also went up against Beit El; and the Lord was with them. And the house of Joseph sent to spy out Beit El. (Now the name of the city was formerly Luz.) And the spies saw a man coming out of the city, and they said to him, "Pray, show us the way into the city, and we will deal kindly with you." And he [the Canaanite] showed them the way into the city; and they smote the city with the edge of the sword, but they let the man and all his family go. And the man went to the land of the Hitttes and built a city, and called its name Luz; that is its name to this day". (Judges 1- 22,26)

30 Understanding and practicing Jerusalem of the Mind prayer/meditation does not directly benefit from the case studies and growing anecdotal data

surrounding DMT for another important reason. From a traditional Torah and Kabbalah perspective getting conscious of one's consciousness and having first hand experiences of the divine is of no value—and is potentially counterproductive—if one does not have the extensive maps that only in-depth and lengthy study of Torah-based Kabbalah supplies. Entering alien territory without your Torah GPS at best leaves one with more questions than answers, as has been well documented by those who have traveled this route. The practitioner may now know there is something else very profound going on here in reality, but like Neo in the movie *The Matrix*, he will not be able to put his finger on it without outside knowledge.

Additionally, this quote from the late Terrence McKenna, perhaps the leading world expert on DMT (among many other disciplines) should be noted, ""I have dreams in which I smoke DMT, and it works. To me that's extremely interesting, because it seems to imply that one does not have to smoke DMT to have the experience. You only have to convince your brain that you have done this, and it then delivers this staggering altered state". Terrence McKenna, *The Archaic Revival*, HarperSanFrancisco, 1991, p. 210.

31 *Marharil Diskin*, (1818–1898, quoted in *Siddur HaGra* brought in the ArtScroll commentary on the Book of Ezekiel), suggests a simple resolution to the apparent contradiction as to whether the Third Temple will be constructed by God or by man. The Third Temple will, in fact, be made out of "fire" and miraculously descend from "above", but it will be missing essential parts that will then require human production to complete it from below. Aside from inherent problems with this solution, the direction taken in Jerusalem of the Mind is altogether a different and deeper inter-dimensional approach. This approach is also predicated upon the advanced exegetical rule that, "Without the *sod*/secret," the Gaon of Vilna said, "the simple meaning is simply not true."

32 *Midrash Rabbah* 68:9

33 There is an additional significance to Jacob's vision that actually lays at the bedrock of the scientific research concerning the pineal gland and it relationship to Peniel — the P2P equation. Regarding the significance of Jacob's "ladder" the Gaon of Vilna has stated, "It is impossible to climb a ladder whose top

reaches towards the heavens without first stepping on the rungs of the ladder that are stationed near the earth. This is the essential idea that was conveyed to our father Jacob in his vision of the ladder." (Quoted by his disciple Hillel of Shklov in *Kol HaTor, Sha'ar Be'er Sheva*, near the end of section 10.) The full context of this quote is found in my *Secret Doctrine of the Gaon of Vilna*, Volume I, p. 146. In other words, similarly it is impossible to grasp the full implications of spiritual truth without understanding its relationship to scientific fact.

34   *Midrash Pirkie diRebbi Eliezer*, chapter 35. Exegetically, the Midrash assumes that Jacob did not bring any anointing oil with him as he himself states the material possessions he had with him when he had begun this particular journey (verse 32:11): "But [only] with my staff I crossed the Jordan [river]". From an esoteric Torah view, every case in Scripture where oil is being poured upon a rock altar, it is done in order to effect unification between higher and lower dimensions. Fundamentally, the oil is a vehicle for an aspect of higher-dimensional consciousness (*mohin*) that is now uniting with the rock, which is an aspect of female essence (*malchut/nukbah*). (For details and additional sources see note by R' David Luria (Radal), PDRE loc. cit.). In simple terms, this means that an aspect of expanded consciousness was opened and a *tikun* was made at that time by Jacob with the Foundation Stone—personally and collectively—and for all future generations.

Jacob was consciously stimulating the higher-dimensional pineal (i.e., of Adam) reciprocally with his personal human pineal. As known, "Nothing descends from Above unless it is initially aroused from below". This principle applies to all acts of *karbanot*/offerings and to prayer and this is the case here as well. Jacob was consciously orchestrating a cosmic *tikun* of the higher-dimensional pineal/Peniel coordinate within the soul of Adam via his vision, erecting the altar from the "rock(s)" upon which his head had been in contact with and then anointing it. Another Midrash (BR, loc. cit.) informs us that, contrary to what would have been expected, the anointing oil was a very small quantity, specifically only enough to fill "the mouth of a jar". Normally, oil is poured or smeared upon much of the length of the pillar, which is paralleling the length of the spinal column (*yesod*). This celestial liquid generated here was specifically only enough to anoint the top of the pillar. In the context of the P2P Principle, the reason for this is clear. The pineal gland and its higher-dimensional correspondence, although it is the *malchut*/kingdom aspect relative to what is above it, relative to us it is the head or crown of our cerebrospinal structure below. Jacob was specifically anointing, i.e., "squeezing the rock", so to speak, of the analogous DMT liquid from the *keter*/crown/pineal/Peniel.

35 Psalms 137: 5, 6. This psalm, during weekdays, is recited before *Berkat HaMazon* (Grace after meals). Indeed, the custom that a bridegroom places ashes upon his head under the *chupah*/canopy before the actual marriage ceremony is derived from this verse (Rama, *Orach Chaim* 360). On a simple level (*pshat*) the expression "If I forget you, O Jerusalem, let my right [hand] forget [its skill]" is referring historically to the professional Levite musicians. Upon being conquered and captured by the Babylonians during the destruction of the First Temple, they voluntarily cut off their own thumbs so that they could not be forced to play their harps and other string instruments for the pleasure and amusement of their conquerors. The verse, however, literally reads, "If I forget you, O Jerusalem, let my right forget". From the perspective of the inner Torah (the Kabbalah) this is referring to the known axiom that the divine "constricting powers" which emanate from the "left side" (the *gevurot*) must always be sweetened and mitigated by the divine "expanding powers" which emanate from the "right side" (the *hasadim*). The spiritual water — the Living Liquid — that flows out from beneath the "threshold of the house" (the Holy of Holies) at the center of Jerusalem is, for the Nation of Israel, the only true source of that mitigation. If the purpose and secret of Jerusalem is "forgotten", then the direct flow (the "right side") is cut off and the powers of constriction implode on themselves with no "coolant" to water them down and transform them. This explains the following verse, "Let my tongue cling to my palate if I fail to recall you". Moisture within the body is produced from the "waters of the *hasadim*". The tongue clings to a parched palate when there is not sufficient liquid (saliva) to mitigate the dryness, i.e., when there are no expanding energies (the *hasadim*) that emanate from the "right side" of Jerusalem to mix with the constricting energies (the *gevurot*). (R' Moshe David Valli (colleague and disciple of the Ramchal) in his commentary on Psalms, loc. cit.)

36　*Shulchan Aruch, Orach Chayim*, section 94. Additionally, in the following section 95:2 the *S.A.* states, "...and one should imagine as if he is standing in the *Beit HaMikdash*". The terminology of the Tur (quoted by the *Kaf HaChayim*, 94, note 3) is, "It is considered as if we are standing and praying within it [the Mikdash].

37　*Kitzur Shulchan Aruch* 18:10. The *Kaf haChaim* (Orach Chaim 94:1:4 citing Radvaz Vol. 2; Ch. 648) rules that if a Jew was forced onto the Temple Mount and the time of prayer arrived while he's standing between the Western Wall and the place of the Holy of Holies, "he should pray facing towards the Holy of Holies even though his back will be facing the Western Wall."

38　Ibid, subsection 3.

39　In the last two centuries and especially in the last few decades other sections and archeological artifacts of the First and Second Temples have since been unearthed.

40　Ratzlav-Katz, Nissan (July 23, 2007). "100,000 Jews at Western Wall for Tisha B'Av 5767". Arutz Sheva http://www.israelnationalnews.com/News/News. aspx/123174.

41　Judith Weil. "Kosel Visitors record", *Jewish Tribune*, 22 October, 2010.

42　In 2000, Pope John Paul II placed a letter in the wall and in July 2008, U.S. Presidential candidate Barack Obama placed a written prayer in the wall.

43　Tractate *Middot* 2:1

44　Eicha Rabba (Midrash on Lamentations) 1:31.

45　Similarly, based upon these same principles it is an ancient Jewish custom that when possible one's bed should be placed along an east-west axis with one's head facing east. This is replicating the original higher-dimensional directional alignment of Adam at the time of his creation, as is known.

46　*Otzrot Ramchal Likutim* p. 251. Similarly, the Ramchal's close friend and colleague writes, "The matter of the Shechinah that remains at the Western Wall and never departs from there is literally the same [i.e., a fractal iteration] as the "vapor of the bones" (R' Moshe David Valli, *Sefer HaLikutim, p.* 355.)

47　The points along this meridian, from most outward to the most inward, are known by the Talmudic Sage-Mystics as the Luz cave (the occiput), the Luz bone (the atlas) and the Luz essence (the pineal DMT). (*Etzem* — literally meaning both bone and essence).

48   In the Torah tradition, it is known that our entire planet is interlaced with a network of circuits that all have their common root in Jerusalem from whence they fan out to the whole world. King Solomon was able to access this hidden landscape. Everything that King Solomon directed and constructed in the "lower Jerusalem" was paralleling precisely its corresponding root in the higher-dimension Jerusalem (see e.g., R' Moshe David Valle in his commentary on Kohelet) .In the Book of Ecclesiastics (Kohelet 2:5), King Solomon wrote, concerning the physical and spiritual architectural design that he developed for the capital city of Jerusalem, "I made gardens and orchards and I planted in them all kinds of fruits". Upon this verse the Midrash (Tanchuma *Kedoshim* 10) elaborates:

> Solomon literally planted every kind of fruit tree, even the pepper tree [as one example of exotic vegetation that does notgrow indigenously in the land of Israel]. All fertility derives from Zion/*Tziyon* [i.e., the Foundation Stone] which was the co-ordinate from which the world was created. From Zion *gidim* (lit., veins, meridians, arteries or nerves) emanate to all the countries of the world and carry the ability to produce each country's unique produce. Solomon, in his surpassing wisdom, knew where to find each of those veins in the vicinity of Jerusalem and planted the appropriate tree. For example, on the vein going to Kush (often identified as Ethiopia) he planted pepper trees — and they all produced. This is why the prophet (Ezekiel 31:12) refers to Eretz Yisrael as "the navel of the world", for Eretz Yisrael, like the navel of a fetus, is the place where the cord that provides it with life and nourishment is attached.

The Midrash (Ecclesiastes Rabba 2:4) also states, "Solomon in his wisdom stood upon the center [lit., "foundation", from the same root as *shetiya*, i.e., the *Even Shetiya*/Foundation Stone] and saw which root branched off to there [particular countries]. He planted upon the root of that country and in this way produced fruit". (The Midrash here also adds the tradition that, from another perspective, "Solomon made use of *ruchot* (spirits/demons) and sent them to India from where they brought him water with which to water [the pepper trees] here [in the land of Israel] and it produced fruit").

These inner-dimensional circuits apparently may also be alluded to in the Talmudic reference to the "underground tunnels" through which the *tzadikim*, who are buried outside of Eretz Yisrael, will "roll" their way back to be resurrected in the Land of Israel (Talmud *Yavamot* 111a, also in conjunction to Ezekiel 37:12).

49 These axioms, principals and applications are explained and developed at length in the classic, authoritative work *Nefesh HaChayim* (The Living Soul) especially in Gate 1, by the Talmudic Sage-Mystic R' Chayim Volozhin, the most illustrious student of the Gaon of Vilna.

50 The master Talmudic Sage-Mystic, R' Shlomo Eliyashev, wrote in the beginning of the 20th century, "Behold, in truth at that period [of space and time before the collapse of Adamic consciousness and reality] the entirety of the Diaspora (lit., *chutz laAretz*, i.e., all territory outside of the borders of Israel) also had the sanctity (*kedusha*) of the current Land of Israel.... Therefore, this being the case behold, [at the stage of reality before the Adamic dimensional collapse] there was no aspect whatsoever of the depreciation of countries outside of Israel [i.e., nothing existed *outside* of the Garden of Eden — the higher-dimensional root of Eretz Yisrael]. The entirety of the [present] Diaspora had the original sanctity of the Land of Israel. This will also be the case in the future [Messianic Era] as it is written in the Midrash (*Pesikta Rabbati* section 1), 'In the future Eretz Yisrael will be as the entirety of the whole world'. ... Likewise, [if not for the consumption of the Tree of Knowledge] it would have been the case with the reality of the world; its entirety also would only be the holiness of the Land of Israel. (*Leshem Dayah*, Part II, *Drush* 3, *Anaf* 12, p. 56. See also, *Leshem Dayah*, Part II, *Drush* 3, *Anaf* 15, p. 62 and *Leshem Dayah*, Part II, *Drush* 4, *Anaf* 12, siman 10, p. 116).

There are multitudes of rabbinic statement-formulas to this effect that in the higher-dimensional messianic future Jerusalem will literally be everywhere as all reality will reveal itself to be only aspects of the original higher-dimensional Israel, Jerusalem, the Temple and the Foundation Stone! Another example is (*Esther Rabba* 1:4), "As the Shechinah (Divine Presence) spreads from the Temple to throughout Jerusalem, so will the Shechinah one day fill the world from one end to the other, as it is written, 'And may the whole world be filled with His glory, Amen and Amen' (Psalms 72:19).

51 Likewise, another common example is water. Water reaches its boiling point at 212 degrees Fahrenheit and it freezes at 32 degrees Fahrenheit. Water will not boil at 211 degrees nor will it freeze at 33 degrees (varying with pressure and other factors). It is that one iota of additional heat or cold which "pushes" it over the edge into a different quality, a different reality. A related model to the "Horton metaphor" is known as the "Hundredth Monkey" phenomenon (Although there are those who maintain that the source of this reported empirical observation is an urban legend). Related concepts, all with newly coined terms, are Sheldrake"s "morphic fields", Dawkins' "meme" and Gladstone's "tipping point."

52 "This letter "*yud*" [of the Tetragrammaton and all of its iterations] is the *Even Shetiya* from where the world was formulated. Concerning it, it is written, 'The stone which the builders have rejected has become the Head Stone'". (*Tikuney HaZohar, tikun* 63 with the glosses of the Gra).

53 The Jebusites were one of the accursed Canaanite nations that Israel was commanded to destroy. Any of the Canaanite tribes, however, always had the option to repudiate idolatry, accept the Seven Universal Noachide Laws. This was the case with Araunah the Jebusite. (See Radak at the end of II Samuel for a simple narrative explanation).

54 There are other *pshat* (i.e., simple narrative) explanations of the unexpected Scriptural identification of Araunah being a "king", but his role as the "*Nogah* King of the Noahides" is the Torah's deeper intent.

55 The cosmic connection of Araunah with the Foundation Stone is further evidenced by a strange statement of the sages. When the Jews, following the destruction of the First Temple, retuned from Babylonia they found buried

beneath the altar of the Temple the skull of Araunah. Another version has it that King Hezekiah found the skull (Jerusalem Talmud *Sotah* 23b, *Pesachim* 36b). In the classical fashion of the Talmudic Sage-Mystics, they reveal apparent mundane matters, even at times appearing implausible, in order to conceal secrets. (In this case, Araunah had lived over 500 years prior to the return from the exile, how did his "skull" end up under the holy altar when a dead body confers impurity and how did they know it was his skull?). Minimally, the sages are clearly alluding to a holy essence rooted in the "skull/ brain" of Araunah, the *ger toshav*, that continued to play an important role in the Temple service and that would continue for future generations as well. Possibly, the vital Noahide role in the redemption process has come full circle from the past to the future and that future is now.

There is yet another crucial connection for non-Jews in the secret of the "The Head of Esau," the twin brother of Jacob. This will require, however, a separate chapter of its own in a future version of this work.

PART II: Keys to the Kingdom

Entering the City of Luz,
the New Jerusalem and Beyond

Part II of *The Jerusalem Stone of Consciousness* presents additional transmissions from the Talmudic Sage-Mystics concerning the mystery behind three distinct ancient cities, each one called Luz. As detailed below, the Rabbinic Masters of Concealment have, astoundingly, handed down actual keys in order to enter the inner Kingdom of Luz. Moreover, they are virtually pointing the direction to go and handing us the maps as well. A path lost for years will open to any sincere seeker of truth and higher Torah consciousness. It is, however, an ornate multi-dimensional map with ascending levels of complexity and coherency, ever drawing one into deeper and more profound inner visions. Here, in Part II, in addition to what has been explained in Part I, specific meditative/consciousness techniques are presented that lead to the Inner Jerusalem of the Mind.[1]

The "Other Kabbalah"

As known, the term "kabbalah" refers to the esoteric Jewish tradition. The word literally means "received", i.e., that which has been handed down and received through an unbroken tradition from master to disciple. Although not widely known, originally the term Kabbalah referred to the entirety of the Oral tradition as it was originally forbidden to write down that which was meant to remain only oral in nature and not written. The entire Oral Torah was the living kabbalah/tradition as it was that which had been handed down and received through an unbroken tradition. After much of the Oral Torah was written down beginning in the second century after the Common Era, the most hidden and secretive parts of the Oral Torah — the esoteric Jewish tradition — was then uniquely designated as the Kabbalah.

However, it is even less known (outside of Talmudic circles), that long before the vast corpus of the Oral Torah was permitted to be written down, the original usage of the term kabbalah referred specifically to all the other books of the Torah outside of the Chumash (Five Books of Moses/Pentateuch.) The Chumash was the Torah proper and the remaining 19 books — the Prophets and the Writings — were uniquely designated as "Words of Kabbalah", a living tradition also rooted in the Sinaic revelation. Simply speaking, this was done to distinguish the supreme sanctity of the Chumash from the relatively lesser sanctity and authority of the "Nach" (*Neviim*/Prophets and *Ketuvim*/Writings). The fact, however, that the books of the Prophets and the Writings were the original "kabbalah" allows us to draw our attention to a little known truth about the Kabbalah — the hidden wisdom of Israel.

Long before the permissibility of writing down the secrets of the Torah, where did the Torah sages conceal their ancient legacy of hermetically sealed "mysteries of creation"? Astoundingly, the masters of concealment encrypted their secret knowledge in the very text of the books of the Prophets and Writings! These secrets, however, remain totally camouflaged and utterly inaccessible without the extremely sophisticated encryption codes. Those codes themselves, in turn, are buried in the last place virtually anyone would think to look — in the Aggadah portions of the Talmud. These sections — which comprise more than a quarter of the otherwise legal and ritual discussions of the sixty volumes of the Talmud — include often strange and seemingly outlandish remarks and commentaries on scriptural verses. There are thousands of such encryptions and what they secreted in their "commentary" on the following passage from the Book of Judges is one of them.[2] Although even less obvious, this cryptological methodology is all the more so with Scripture itself. The rule is that the Torah and those initiated into her depths, i.e., Written and the Oral Torahs interfaced with each other, "Reveal a handbreadth while concealing two handbreadths". With the most profound secrets they "Reveal a handbreadth and conceal a thousand handbreadths" and that is the case here with the secret of the three cities of Luz.

1. Keys to the Kingdom:
The Three Cities of Luz

There exists a commonly known city-place in the Torah called Beit El who's original name was Luz. This is the location of Jacob's visionary dream and the future temples. This site of Beit El/Luz, its interface with the Foundation Stone, Peniel and Jacob's theurgic orchestration that he affected there, is discussed at length in Part I of *The Jerusalem Stone of Consciousness — Kabbalah, the Pineal Gland & Jerusalem of the Mind*. Here again is this pivotal passage from Genesis 28-10, 22:

> Jacob left Beer Sheva and headed toward Charan. He encountered *the place* and spent the night there, because the sun had set; he took of the stones of *the place* and arranged them about his head and lay down to sleep in *that place*. He had a vision in a dream and behold, a ladder was set upon the earth and its top reached heavenward; and behold! Angels of God were ascending and descending upon it [or upon Jacob]. Behold, God was standing over him ... Jacob awoke from his sleep and said, "Indeed God is in *this place* and I was unaware". He became alarmed and he said, "How awesome is *this place*, it can only be the House of God and this is the gate of the heavens". Jacob arose early in the morning and took the

stone that he had placed around his head and set it up as a pillar; then he poured oil on its top". He named the place Beit El (House of God or God's Temple). *The town's original name, however, had been Luz.*

Jacob's city of Luz, however, is not the only city with the name Luz. In fact, there exists, not only one other city in the Torah called Luz but there are actually *two* other cities called Luz! These two other cities called Luz are not as commonly known because they are not in the *Chumash* (Five Books of Moses/Pentateuch), but in the "*Nach*" (*Neviim*/Prophets and *Ketuvim*/Writings) portion of the "*Tanach*". Specifically, these two other cities of Luz are mentioned in the books of the Prophets.

> As we will be dealing with three different cities named Luz each with its own unique narrative, for clarity's sake we will refer to Jacob's city of Luz as (0) indicating the Original Luz, i.e., the first city of Luz that appears in the Torah. The two other cities of Luz that will now be introduced will be designated as Luz (1) and Luz (2).

Be prepared, as it will become evident that all three cities of Luz are, in fact, three aspects of a singular *super*-city: the Kingdom of Luz. For the one who desires to take this cosmic "treasure map" seriously, know that trying to coherently juggle and decode three different cities each with the same name can be very challenging. (Think of it akin to a 4-Dimensional board game, only that the stakes here are as high as they can get— both figuratively and literally).

The Book of Judges informs us that:

The House of Joseph also went up against Beit El; and the Lord was with them. And the house of Joseph sent to spy out *Beit El. Now the name of the city was formerly Luz.* And the spies saw a man coming out of the city, and they said to him, "Pray, show us the way into the city, and we will deal kindly with you." And he [the Canaanite] showed them the way into the city; and they smote the city with the edge of the sword, but they let the man and all his family go. *And the man went to the land of the Hittites and built a city, and called its name Luz; that is its name to this day.* (Judges 1-22, 26)

In commenting on this passage[3], the Talmudic Sage-Mystics start out simply enough with what is a lesson in ethical behavior and "spiritual etiquette". They teach that the reward one earns, by escorting a guest on his way or even directing someone looking for his correct destination, is inestimable, as is illustrated in this episode from the Book of Judges. What is the connection?

As related in the verses, during that time in history, the Israelite nation was in the process of conquering the Canaanite cities in the land of Israel. One such Canaanite city was called Beit El, formally known as Luz (1), and was located in the territory of Joseph's sons, Ephraim and Manasseh — the "House of Joseph". The ancient Canaanite city of Beit El/Luz (1) was unique in that it was impenetrable because it had a secret entrance that was hidden from all outsiders. Men from the House of Joseph were sent as scouts to hide out in the vicinity. They waited until a Canaanite man emerged from within the walls and they captured him. They assured him that neither he nor his family would be harmed if he revealed to them the location of the secret entrance to the city. The Canaanite agreed and he and his family were protected and saved in the conquest that ensued. The man and his family then went off to the land of the Hittites and built there a new city, which he named Luz (2) after the name of the first Luz (1) and, "that is its name to this day".

The Canaanite who directed the Hebrew warriors to the

concealed entrance to Luz (1) had, in effect, "escorted" them to their destination. His reward for even this small act of escorting, not only delivered him and his family from certain death, but his generations afterwards were blessed, as they were the builders and citizens of the unique second city of Luz (2).

Throughout the Talmud, Midrash and Zohar the sages paint a picture of these "twin cities" both called Luz (1 & 2). Both cities abound with what appears on the surface to be legends which more than challenge our rational thinking. The first city of Luz (1), as explained, was hidden from outsiders and even seasoned warriors could not penetrate its hermetically sealed exterior. The oral tradition amplifies this in numerous places by informing us that the singular passage to Luz (1) was camouflaged by the foliage of a hazelnut tree (*luz* in Hebrew[4]) whose hollowed out trunk led into a cave (the "Luz cave" discussed further below) that led into a tunnel that led into the city.

The second city of Luz (2) was impervious to destruction by conquering nations and its inhabitants continuously lived as a cohesive community throughout the millennia and were neither driven from their home nor ever assimilated or lost their unique purpose. The holiness of this city of Luz had the distinction of being the location where the material for the priestly garments was dyed, the extremely valuable royal blue *techeilit* of Israel and the ancient Middle East.[5] One who entered Luz was infused with the desire to perform mitzvot (good actions) and acts of kindness. The second City of Luz (2) was also known as "Kushta" — Aramaic for "Truth" for the inhabitants lived in pure truth and could never tell a lie.[6] Luz (2) was so unique that even the Angel of Death did not have permission to enter. When the elderly of Luz (2) grew weary of their eternal existence they would go outside the walls to die and depart from the world.[7]

It is no coincidence that the Canaanite's first city of Beit El/Luz recorded here in Judges has exactly the same double names as Jacob's city of Luz (0). What becomes clear is that in their essence they are one and the same, i.e., various aspects of one inter-dimensional coordinate. This is despite the fact that on the geographical plane these two cities do not appear to be the same at all. Jacob's Luz (0), the site of the Foundation Stone and the two Temples, was in the territory of Benjamin (and Judah[8]) and the episode in Judges with the Canaanite's Luz (1) was in the territory of Ephraim, to the north of Jerusalem. But this is the way of Torah — both the written and the oral — that it often reveals certain matters in order to conceal more information within those very matters it reveals. Additionally, there is now another city with the name Luz (2) that was built in "the land of the Hittites" by the Canaanite.

To review, the three Luz keys to the Kingdom of Luz that the combined Written and Oral Torahs have transmitted to us are (In the chronological order they appear in Scripture):

1) The Original City of Luz of Jacob's *Makom*/Place of the Foundation Stone (and all that is associated there with it, e.g., his vision and its extensive ramifications, the "ladder", the "oil", the future temples, the Holy of Holies and the Ark of the Covenant.[9]

2) The City of Luz of the Luz tree and its camouflaged secret entrance to the cave and the tunnel (as well as the Canaanite's secret method of how to "turn" the key to enter the tunnel, as explained below).

3) The City of Luz also known as Kushta located and built by the same Canaanite. It is an earth-

ly Garden of Eden permeated by truth, indestructibility and perpetual life and "that is its
name to this day".

As explained above, the prophets and their disciples — the
Talmudic Sage-Mystics who were the recipients of their living
legacy — reveal ostensibly little pebbles of information in order
to conceal beneath them great mountains of esoteric data and
higher- dimensional maps. In this case, it is what they are concealing beneath the leaves of a hallowed out hazelnut tree. The great
16th century Talmudic Sage-Mystic, the Maharal of Prague,
maintains that the reference to the Canaanite's second city of
Luz (2) is, in fact, the location of the Jacob's original Beit El/Luz
(0)![10] The city associated with the royal blue *techeilet* dye, never
to have been destroyed, never having had its inhabitants dis-
persed as well as its denizens being impervious to death, is none
other than the Luz of the Foundation Stone (0).

Nevertheless, the identification of the Canaanite's second Luz
with Jacob's Luz (0), the site of the future temples, appears to fly in
the face of the verse that explicitly states, "And the man went to
the land of the Hittites and built a city and called its name Luz (2);
that is its name to this day."[11] This verse, however, appearing as it
does to lead us far away from the original Beit El/Luz (0), is precisely
so. Scripture *intentionally* tells us that the Canaanite's second city of
Luz (2) was built far away in a foreign land. Rather, the concluding
verse in this episode is an intentional decoy to keep the path to Luz
and beyond privy only to the initiated.

Yet, any analysis of a scriptural verse, whether it be on the
simple narrative level or (and even more so) on the esoteric
level must adhere to the exegetical rule that, "No scriptural
verse can be divorced from its literal meaning". So which is it?
Can the second city of Luz (2) be both inside the borders of

Israel and outside at the same time?! Yes. This is precisely the intention of the Torah and her sages. Even though we are building upon the Maharal's identification of the unique, other-worldly qualities of the Canaanite's second city of Luz (2) with Jacob's city of Luz (0), there is still something, or some aspect, of the second Luz that appears to remain outside of the Land of Israel. To the contrary, a crucial aspect of the Canaanite's second city of Luz (2) *must* be located outside of the Land of Israel in a "foreign land"! This is in order for the Torah to "reveal and conceal" the esoteric formula that there are, in fact, two Luz openings, a double entrance to the secret of Luz!

The identification of the new Luz (2) with Jacob's Luz (0) resolves another difficultly. Where is Luz today? Specifically, where are each of the three cities of Luz located? The location of Jacob's Luz (0) is definitively the Temple mount and the Foundation Stone. With regard as to the location, however, of the Canaanite's first city of Luz which was conquered by the tribe of Joseph, there is no consensus as to its geographical coordinates. Although the verse clearly situates it in the territory north of Jerusalem, according to tradition no such place name with Luz exists to this day (nor according to archeological excavation). The absence of an original location of the Canaanite's first city of Luz, however, poses no problem, as its geographical location, from the perspective of the Torah, is no longer relevant.

The geographical location, however, of the Canaanite's second city of Luz (2) is problematic. Outside of the Land of Israel there is no city by the name of Luz nor has there ever been such a place name recorded.[12] Yet, the text states, "that is its name to this day". Rashi writes that wherever it is stated in Tanach "Until this day", 'the intention is literally forever'".[13] It should now be evident that the Canaanite's second city of Luz (2) is not so much a "city" as it is a portal *into* a city and that city is the New Jerusalem built upon the Foundation Stone of creation. Luz is a "way station" and an actual "place", more specifically the transitional "space" *between* dimensions. "And the man went to the land of the Hittites and built a city, and called its name Luz; that is its name to this day". Where is the Canaanite's second city of Luz? Luz is literally referring to the esoteric collection of interfacing teachings from the Talmudic Sage-Mystics that all map out the deeper truth of Luz.

Torah and the Talmudic Sage-Mystics, as known, speak simultaneously on the *pshat*/narrative level and on the *sod*/secret level. On the *pshat* level the second city of Luz (2) *is* outside the Land of Israel and the intention of Scripture was to seemingly locate it far way in order to camouflage its secrets from the uninitiated. On the *sod*/secret level, however, the "outer Luz" (2) is isomorphic with Jacob's City of Luz (0). The double character of this second Luz city is exact because a city of Luz is concealing the secret of the requisite double entrance to Luz, i.e., the Canaanites second "outer" Luz being the gateway to the first. This is a crucial component behind the Torah's intention of the two cities both being called Luz, one being external (2) and one being internal (0) to the spiritual nature of the Land of Israel. Thus, the *pshat* and the *sod* are also now literally isomorphic one with the other, as they always should be.[14]

The "outer" and more external nature of the second Luz (2) is evident both from the fact that it was outside of the Land of Israel and by the fact that it was inhabited by the amoral and perverse pagan based Canaanites.[15] In other words, the secret of Luz, in all of its manifestations and on every level, is forever polarized with two terminals — positive and negative relative to each other. In its essence, Luz is simultaneously spiritual and earthly, holy and profane, inner and outer, within the Land of Israel and outside of the Land of Israel, the first city of Luz (1) and the second city of Luz (2), at the top of the spine and at the base of the spine. This polarity, running along a common axis, is alluded to by the rabbinic term *luz shel ha-shidrah*, the "luz of the spine"[16], as explained more below.[17]

The fact that the first Luz was destroyed and is no longer in existence is indicating that it is only its essence that remains which is now reunited with Jacob's Luz (0). Also, as mentioned above, Jacob's Beit El/Luz (0) and the Canaanite's first city of Beit El/Luz (1) intentionally both have exactly the same "double name". They are intrinsically connected and each one contains information that the other is lacking. Now, in addition, the second city of Luz (2) is an extension of the first city of Luz (1). Both, in turn, are to be identified with Jacob's Luz (0)![18] (This can be formulated as (0)=(1)=(2)=(0)). The entirety of the three cities of Luz now constitutes a *Kingdom* of Luz. The whole wondrous secret of the Kingdom of Luz is even greater than its amazing individual city parts. This secret has been so ingeniously guarded and hidden that it requires *three* keys to open it up and *all* three must be used simultaneously. The three cities of Luz are like transparencies layered one upon the other, each one revealing more details until the full picture emerges. The Gate to Heaven — the vortex into higher dimensionality and a step into the true messianic era — can only be accessed when the three Luz locations and their unique qualities are superimposed one upon the other.

All three Luz keys are three distinct fragments of one sacred "treasure map" plotting out and directing us towards a single co-ordinate. There is, however, an additional fourth key to the Kingdom of Luz. Well known to the Talmudic Sage-Mystics there is yet *another* Luz phenomenon! Without the knowledge of this fourth key one cannot enter into the mystery of the Kingdom of Luz even with the three Luz keys described so far. This is because the fourth aspect of Luz is not a key per se; rather the fourth Luz is the very *keyhole* through which the secret of the three keys must be inserted! This keyhole is in the reach of all of us yet it is located in the last place anyone would think to look.

2. Keyhole to the Kingdom:
The Luz Bone

Unless one has studied in a yeshiva (rabbinic college), has a Jewish scholarly education or comes from a very traditional Jewish environment, most Jews cannot recall any Biblical city called Luz. This is despite the fact that there are three cities of Luz clearly mentioned in Scripture. Most traditional Jews, however, have heard about another "luz". It is not a city per se but rather it is a feature of the human body. It is known as the "luz bone" and the "luz of the spine" (or vertebral column). All Torah authorities, past and present, agree that it is from this bone located in the spine that the human body is reconstructed at the time of the great Resurrection of the Dead.[19]

As explained in Part I of *The Jerusalem Stone of Consciousness*, when a person dies, the various levels of the soul (in descending order they are the *chaiyah*, *neshamah* and *ruach*), return to their respective extra-dimensional roots. The lowest level of the soul, the *nefesh*, remains with the corpse until the body decays and disintegrates. The *nefesh* then also returns to its source leaving only the bones in the grave. There remains, however, a field of dormant life-energy that "sleeps" with the bones and never departs. This force, in the language of the Talmudic Sage-Mystics, is known as *"havla d'garmay"*, "breath" or "vapor of the bones" and it is from this "vapor of the bones" that the soul, together with the body, is "cloned", as it were, and reconstituted in the final Resurrection back into its original, and now perfected state. Ramchal writes: [20]

> There remains in the grave of a person a bone which is called "luz". Through it the body will be reconstructed at the time of the Resurrection of the Dead. There also remains [in the bone(s)] a portion of the *nefesh* which is called "the vapor of the bones" (*havlay d'garmay*). Likewise, in the case of the Temple there remains the Western Wall.[21]

The west of one's body is — as known in the Kabbalah — the back of one's head. It is known that the *Shechinah* dwells in the west. (The *Shechinah* is the term the Talmudic Sage-Mystics use to refer to any spatial-temporal aspect of the Divine. She is Divinity's lower dimensional immanent Self, while He is Her corresponding aspect of transcendent Divinity). Therefore, the *Shechinah* dwells in the back of the head. The west and back of the head of a person is also the location of the mysterious "luz bone", a type of inter-dimensional coordinate from which one's true eternal body(s) and soul(s) are "reconstituted" at the time of the great Resurrection (i.e., the point of intersection between *"Olam HaZeh"* and *"Olam HaBah.* This is the ultimate reunion of lower and higher-dimensionality).

Concerning the intrinsic connection between the city of Luz and the luz bone, a Torah master from the last century wrote,[22] "The explanation of this matter... [of the city of Luz and its primeval connection to the Hebrew letter *tet* (also representing the number 9) as explained at length in the Zohar, *Terumah* 74b] is a great esoteric and obscure secret from the mysteries of the Torah...this is the wondrous secret why the sages called the bone that is indestructible and remains in the grave the luz bone. It is from that bone that a person will be resurrected and it is that bone that is alive and exists for eternity. They called it the "luz of the spine". Likewise, that city called Luz is where no man dies but rather lives forever, for the esoteric reasons given [in the Zohar and elsewhere]. It was named Luz because of the bone that is called luz which lives forever."[23]

Ostensibly, the luz bone is designated by the Talmudic Sage-Mystics as the luz of the spine to distinguish it from the city (or cities) of Luz. The fact, however, that the same name is used for both cannot escape us. From the perspective of Jerusalem of the Mind the three cities of Luz and the luz bone are, in fact, inseparable. This is true to the extent that if the three cities of Luz constitute a single key to the kingdom of heaven, as explained above, the luz bone and its location is the *keyhole* to the key to the kingdom, a virtual "stargate" into higher-dimensional consciousness.

Where in the spine is this "inter-dimensional keyhole" located? There are numerous sources that explicitly state that the luz bone is located at the top of the spine, i.e., at the base of the skull. There are, however, various other authoritative sources that clearly identify its location at the base of the spine. The uppermost bone of the spine is the atlas vertebra, whereas the lowest bone in the spine is the coccyx. These two traditions appear to be at two opposite extremes. However, applying the rabbinic formula, "These and those are [both] the words of the living God", it is clear that there have always been two Torah "luz bones", one at the top of the spine and one at the bottom of the spine. Both are true and both are necessary. The two luz bones are replicating a hidden symmetry that is reflecting their higher-dimensional roots in the body of archetypal man — Adam, the template from which the human was "made in the image of God". In other words, by divine design there must be two luz bones in the human body.

So where is the location of the "keyhole" to the secret entrance of the City of Luz? Astoundingly, it is hidden in the last place anyone would think to look — in the back of one's own head! [24] In addition, just as the geographical Luz cave was well camouflaged with leaves from the luz tree so is the entrance to one's own physiological Luz cave concealed under the locks from the hair of the head! But there is even more to this "keyhole" as the two-pronged nature of Luz continues to iterate its dual, polarized nature.

As explained above, the singular passage to the Canaanite's Luz (1) was camouflaged by the foliage of a hazelnut tree whose hollowed out trunk led into a cave — the "Luz cave" — that led into a tunnel that led into the city. It is now evident that the luz bone and the occiput are the physiological analog to the geographical "luz cave". Now, if there are two "luz bones" in the body should it not follow that there should geographically be two luz caves? Precisely so and this is another secret that the Book of Judges encoded within the Canaanite's two cites called Luz (1 & 2). The first Luz (1), also known as Beit El, was located *inside* of the Land of Israel, while the second city of Luz (2) built by the Canaanite was *outside* of the Land of Israel in the "land of the Hittites". The Holy Land Luz (1) functions within a higher spiritual dimension whereas the "Hittite Luz" (2) operates within a lower dimension. The two, however, depend upon each other and, functioning together, create a type of spiritual "double seal". Moreover, the double seal of the two Luzes serves a *double* purpose: A.) It effectively keeps the uninitiated and external forces out and, B.) It contains the secret blueprint for the actual inner technology necessary in order to enter the Kingdom of Luz, as explained further below in Turning the Key: the Torah Torus. But first we need to shed some more light on the luz bone.

Saturday Night Light — The Feast of Luz

The luz bone(s) is quite fundamental to Torah consciousness and the Judaic tradition; it plays a major role in a ritual that has long been a part of Jewish observance: the *Melaveh Malkah*. Aside from the traditional three meals eaten on the Shabbat, it is an ancient custom to arrange a small additional fourth meal on Saturday night in honor of the departure of the Shabbat. This meal is known as the *Melaveh Malkah* — Escorting the [Shabbat] Queen.[25] This meal follows the *Havdalah* ritual that distinguishes the holiness of the Seventh Day from the incoming six days of the week. Now, just as we welcome in the Shabbat on Friday night, we also escort her out following the close of the Shabbat. There are a number of traditions and concepts that weave through this meal based upon the unique field of energy that is present at this time. Here, we will concern ourselves only with that which pertains directly to the luz bone.

The famed sage and legal expert R' Yisrael Meir Kagan HaKohen (Poland 1838-1933), known as the *Chafetz Chaim* (mentioned in Part I, Chapter 8), writes in his authoritative commentary on the Code of Jewish Law:

> The early authorities have said that there is an organ in the human being and its name is *"naskoy"*.[26] This organ remains in the grave until the time of the resurrection, even after all the bones have decayed. This organ does not receive pleasure from any food substance what so-ever except from the meal of the *Melaveh Malkah*.[27]
>
> The reason for this is because this organ did not receive pleasure from the Tree of Knowledge that Adam ate from on the evening before Shabbat. It only receives pleasure from food that is eaten Saturday night. Therefore, it was not decreed upon it to disintegrate even through the process of death.[28]

The luz bone took not from this lower-dimensional reality nor does it presently partake of this lower dimension. What then is its source of sustenance? The ancient traditions inform us that the entirety of Adam's higher-dimensional "bodily" form, as well as his entire consciousness and reality, were spiritually contaminated due to his partaking of the higher-dimensional "fruit" of the Tree of [Dualistic] Knowledge. One organ, however, was not affected by the "Fall" from higher-dimensionality and that is the *etzem haluz*. The word *etzem* can mean either a bone or the essence of something. Here the term is an intentional double entendre referring to both the bone of luz and the essence of Luz. The *etzem haluz* did not "eat" from the Tree of Knowledge of "duality". It remains, in fact, rooted in the original higher-dimensional Tree of Life.[29] This is reflected in the physiological fact that, as explained in Part I, the pineal gland is the only singular organ in the brain and is paralleling the spiritual Luz bone/essence. All the other organs are dual (i.e., having a right and leftlobe) and therefore parallel the Tree of Knowledge of Duality. It was also explained there that the pineal organ interfaces between the body and the soul. The coined term, the "spirit molecule" captures this phenomenon. The pineal in the individual human and the Foundation Stone in global humanity are both "vestigial organs" penetrating into this lower reality from their root above. From this perspective the singular pineal gland is a literal fractured fraction (i.e., fractal) of the actual Tree of Life "protruding" from its higher-dimensional reality into our lower-dimensional anatomical world. The pineal organ growing in the very middle of the brain is the Tree of Life planted in the very middle of the Garden of Eden.

We can now appreciate that the luz bone is much more than a symbolic concept alluding to a belief in the resurrection of the dead and in the immortality of the soul. The luz bone and its iterations bear within themselves the seeds to resurrect one's own consciousness as well as revealing the inner technology of how to activate P2P and Jerusalem of the Mind, both on the personal level and on the global level. The luz bone is part of a cosmic process that is interdependent with the three keys to the Kingdom of Luz. The two Luz vortices also shed a new light on what is, from many perspectives, one of the most challenging tenets of faith for a believer in the God of Israel. This is the belief in the necessity of a Third Temple.

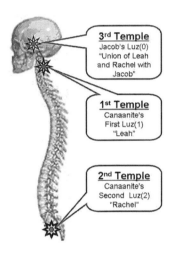

3rd Temple
Jacob's Luz(0)
"Union of Leah
and Rachel with
Jacob"

1st Temple
Canaanite's
First Luz(1)
"Leah"

2nd Temple
Canaanite's
Second Luz(2)
"Rachel"

The Somatic Luz Symmetry of the Three Temples

The secret of the interfacing of the three cities of Luz now allows us a unique insight into the phenomenon of a Third Temple. As introduced in The Riddle of the New Jerusalem in Part I of Jerusalem of the Mind, the existence of a third temple is a cosmological imperative for the entirety of reality for its completion and spiritual evolution. This becomes evident when we again apply the verse/ formula, "From my flesh I will behold God". Whether or not the Third Temple will manifest on the physical or metaphysical plane or an interfacing of both — takes on a radically new perspective when we consider that the global Third Temple has a correspondence to each and every one's individual pineal gland.

As explained, the human body replicating the Divine form, has two major vortices that run along the spine. One is at the base of the head — the "upper Luz" and its iterations — and one at the bottom of the spine — the "lower Luz" and its iterations. These two sacred centers correspond, as explained above, to the two traditions of the location of the Luz bone. They are also known in the Zohar and in Lurianic Kabbalah as "Leah" and "Rachel", the two sister wives of Jacob. Accordingly, the First Temple corresponds to Leah at the base of the head, whereas the Second Temple corresponds to Rachel at the base of the spine. With this symmetrical mapping many biblical verses and rabbinical statements concerning the distinctions between the two Temples become clear. For example, this distinction explains why "miracles" (i.e., extra-dimensional interfacing) were common in the First Temple but were absent in the second Temple and why only in the first Temple (also known as Solomon's Temple) the Holy of Holies housed the *keruvim* (cherubim) and the Ark of the Covenant. This was not, however, the case in the second Temple (also known as Herod's Temple). This was because the aspect of Leah — the "upper" temple — and all of her iterations are rooted in the relatively higher supernal level of the head. On the other hand, Rachel — the "lower" temple — is rooted in the base of the spine (each one, of course, being holographic in nature and therefore containing elements of each other).[30]

If the two temples correlate with the two Luz bones, then which part of the body, made in the higher-dimensional "image" of God, would a Third Temple correspond to? The answer is logical: if we follow the axis that extends along the spine into the middle of the head, we find ourselves right in the middle of the pineal gland. The Third Temple is rooted in the pineal gland, the Gate to Heaven, the portal back to the higher-dimensional Garden of Eden, the Messianic Era and beyond.[31]

The association now of the pineal gland with the Third Temple explains the origin of the rabbinical "dispute", explained in Part I, concerning the nature of the Third Temple: Will it be man-made from below or will it descend from above? There it was explained that, from a meta-physiological perspective, the pineal is the portal through which the life force of the soul enters and leaves the body. The pineal is the seat of consciousness and the bridge which interfaces man with the Divine. Therefore, if the pineal is the nexus between the body and soul, where is it primarily rooted — in the body from below or in the soul from above? The pineal is an organ that fits the template of simultaneously being both the *keter*/crown of the lower dimensional body and the *malchut*/kingdom of the higher-dimensional soul. It is both partially in "this world" and partially in the "next world". Very appropriately has DMT, which hypothetically can be produced by the pineal gland, been identified as a "spirit molecule" — spiritual from above and molecular from below. The Third Temple is also both spiritual from above and physical from below. The kingdom of the three cities of Luz and its unlocking is also the secret to the somatic symmetry of the three temples.

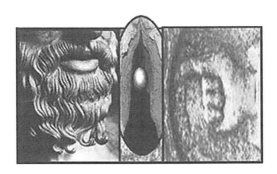

3. Inserting the Key:
How Did He Show Them?

Now that the fourth aspect of Luz — the missing keyhole — has been revealed and integrated, the episode from the Book of Judges has another secret to reveal. The "way into the city" contains more encrypted data, specifically as to *how* to enter into the cave that leads into the tunnel. Surprisingly, it is the Canaanite himself who now teaches us that there are, in fact, *two* Luz portals. These are not, however, in two separate locations but rather they are one *within* the other, a "door within a door"! They are two sets of circular rims or lips one nested within the other. This is the utterly amazing rabbinic secret of the "mouth and the finger" as will now be explained. It is this phenomenon that literally enables us to rediscover the hidden path back into the eternal City of Luz, the Gate of Heaven and onward and inward into the New Jerusalem.

Initially, it appeared that the Canaanite's twin "sister cities" of Luz are legendary tales that may have had some allegorical meaning, or that they once referred to some actual places but are no longer in existence. We see, however, that there is something else quite profound going on here — and it is now going to become even more profound. The episode in the Book of Judges ends by stating, "That is its name to this day". Yet, there is no such city today, certainly not with such fantastical characteristics. This presents a serious quandary. If the words of Torah — and this includes the Book of Judges — emanate from a higher-dimensional divine source (The Divine Mind), they must be as true today as they were the day they were written down. Scripture cannot tell a non-truth and all the more so regarding a city that the sages tell us was also known as *Kushta* — literally meaning "Truth"!

Rather, the City of Luz — synonymous with truth, peace and immortality — is, according to the maps of the Talmudic Sage-Mystics, a spiritual coordinate that *does* exists to this day. The city itself exists in extra-dimensional space-time, i.e., outside of our tangible grasp and even outside of our ability to conceptualize such a reality. The entrance, however, *does* exist in our 3D "Flatland" world. More correctly, the *threshold* to the extra-dimensional city of Luz exists in our 3D world. This is the Talmudic secret of the hollowed luz tree that opens into a cave that leads into a tunnel that leads into Luz (1). It exists in real space-time and it is absolutely accessible "to this day" (Luz 2). This is the selfsame Jacob's Luz (0) which is the Foundation Stone on the Temple Mount. Luz, in the language of the Torah and the sages, is the portal into an inter-dimensional city of light, the Gate to Heaven and the New Jerusalem. It is a state of consciousness as well as an actual coordinate in reality. (On this level, however, "consciousness" and "reality" become indivisible, comprising a single, unified manifold similar to the seamless manifold of space-time). The ancient and unbroken Jewish tradition has even transmitted to us the code of *how* to enter Luz. Now, in our generation — referred to by the Talmudic Sage-Mystics as the Final Generation — every true and serious aspirant has permission to cross this threshold into the Jerusalem of the Mind.

What is the secret to this astounding — and ultimately vital inner technology? The Talmudic commentary concerning the event recorded in the Book of Judges is not over. Rather, following the spiritual-ethical lesson the sages derive from the Canaanite concerning the merit of escorting a visitor or even pointing in the right direction, they present a *machloket* — a classical rabbinic dispute:

> How did he show them [the entrance to the city]? Chizkiyah said, "He twisted his mouth for them [he silently mouthed the directions where the entrance was]". Rabbi Yochanan said, "He showed them [the entrance] with his finger".[32]

On the surface this discussion is very strange. On our own, we would simply assume that when the verse states, "And he showed them the way into the city" that he showed them by taking them directly to the secret entrance. After all, his very life and that of all of his family was in the mercy of his Hebrew captors. Despite this the sages tell us that he, in fact, did not take them to the hidden entrance, but only indicated to them where it was. Yet, apparently the ancient tradition itself was not clear as to the manner in which he did so. "He showed them with his mouth", "No; he showed them with his finger"! But why would he not take them to the opening itself? Ostensibly, according to the commentators he did not because he did not want to put himself in danger, i.e., that his compatriots would see him betraying them, so he only showed them from a distance.

Although possible, attempting to envision these dynamics in actuality appears a bit strained, but leave it as it may be for the moment. However, if the Canaanite did show them without moving his position we would certainly assume he did so by pointing with his finger! That he would have silently mouthed the directions — or alternately, he could have simply "puckered" his lips in the direction — where the entrance was certainly challenges our credulousness! Yet, even assuming that contorting his lips with or without silent words is a possibility, what difference would it make for the following generations of Talmudic masters and their students? All the more so for us — a generation living some 1,600 years later — what possible significance can this rabbinical dispute have for us? Astoundingly, this aggadic transmission is more relevant than we could ever imagine.

It is important to know that the Talmudic Sage-Mystics had a very unique and cryptic language that they spoke and wrote among themselves, especially when transmitting extremely critical keys to the inner Torah blueprints of creation. They were all versed in the same mode of inner-dimensional communication and they knew how to hermetically keep this communiqué away from all but their own colleagues and close initiated disciples. Among many of their formulas is, "These and those are [both] the words of the Living God". The intention is that in virtually every Talmudic era-based "dispute" (including the Mishnah, all the Midrashim, the Zohar and other authoritative works from those periods) both views are correct and both views are necessary for the full picture to emerge. The "finger/mouth" riddle is certainly a case in point. The two sages in our quote knew this axiom well, as did the final redactors of the Talmud, who pieced together and formatted the exact manner in which we have these puzzle pieces today.[33]

In our case of "How did he show them?" how can both views be correct at the same time? This is the secret of passing though the threshold into Luz that the masters of the Kabbalah have handed down to us (The term Kabbalah signifying, as explained above, both the prophetic scriptural tradition and the esoteric tradition). This is exactly their intention; the secret "key" to the eternal City of Luz can *only* be realized when *both* views are superimposed one upon the other generating a third reality. Just as the three cities of Luz only together lead us into the Kingdom of Luz, both the concept of the "mouth" *and* the "finger" must be synthesized together.[34]

Consequently, what the sages are concealing in what they are revealing is neither a "mouth" alone nor a "finger" alone. Yet, it is not *not* a mouth and it is not *not* a finger. Rather, it contains both yet it is more than both. What can that be? What is a "mouth-finger"? The sages are revealing that the "mouth-finger is not a "thing" but rather it is a "method". It is an application of an inner technology with distinct geometrical-like coordinates. It is a tool that can be used to reveal and open the entrance to a timeless "city" that both the Torah and her sages refer to as Luz. If it is real then there must be a real way to get in.

We have now returned full circle to the rather strange *machloket* (rabbinic "dispute"), the apparent difference of opinion between the two Talmudic Sage-Mystics concerning "the mouth and the finger". The "mouth" referred to by the one master is none other than a code word directing us to the occipital "mouth", i.e., the cavity at the back of the head that is covered by the locks of the hair — the foliage of the luz tree! The "finger" of the other master is none other than a code word directing us to a dynamic process of entering the cave by way of a rhythmic "insertion". By gently "pushing" and "pulling" with the power of one's consciousness through the "hole in the tree" — the indentation at the occiput — one can begin to enter into the "luz cave" which leads into the City of Luz. The three cities are the combined "key" to the Kingdom of Luz. The area of the Luz bone at the occiput is the keyhole for the keys to be inserted and the combined "mouth and the finger" is the manner in which the key is "turned". It is this very pulsing rhythmic movement that causes a toroidal space, as explained below, to begin rotating in on itself. The orchestration, however, of "turning" the Luz key is more multifaceted and it requires instruction and practice. This is the Jewish esoteric technology of the Torah Torus introduced below. This, however, requires initiation and this is precisely what the Canaanite "showed" to the Jewish Torah warriors. This is the secret of the Torah Torus.

Deciphering the encoded map of Torah (in this case the verses in the Book of Judges), the sages are transmitting to their disciples and to their disciple's disciples actual blueprints. In this case it is a model that is nothing less than an ancient Torah technology of how to enter the "legendary" city of Luz. What may have begun, however, as appearing as a "legend" is, in fact, something quite real and virtually any serious neophyte can enter. Luz is a real-time inter-dimensional terminal to Peniel, to the Foundation Stone and to the New Jerusalem. Can we access more details of this sacred Torah technology?

Let's return to the Talmud's aggadic discussion above as there is still more buried in its unique cryptological method of transmission. The text quoted above comes with a concluding statement:

> How did he show them? Chizkiyah said, "He twisted his mouth for them". Rabbi Yochanan said, "He showed them with his finger". Another tradition (a *baraita*) supports Rabbi Yochanan, "Because this Canaanite showed them the way with his finger he caused salvation for himself and his descendants onto the end of all generations".

The redactors of the Talmud (the Rabbinic Sage-Mystics from the 3rd to the 5th century C.E.) presumably saw it necessary to bring a separate tradition in order to corroborate Rabbi Yochanan in his apparent opposition to the view of Chizkiyah. They received an oral tradition in the name of the same Rabbi Yochanan that it was indeed the finger of the Canaanite and *not* his mouth that was used. Yet, there is an obvious question here. If, as explained above, that both views are true and only together they comprise a unified whole –"These and those are the words of the Living God" — then the case should be closed. What need would there be to bring additional oral evidence to support the view of Rabbi Yochanan? Moreover, regardless if it was the finger or the mouth no *halachic*/legal difference is obtained. As known, within the rabbinic traditions of non-legal matters of Aggadah and Midrash the apparent conclusions, or absence of conclusions, are not binding as there is no practical or ritualistic application.

Rather, it appears once again that the sages are revealing outer information in order to conceal additional inner information. The unnecessary additional support and quote from Rabbi Yochanan is, in fact, very necessary. With the repetition of the aspect of the "finger", simple math tells us that we now have one "mouth" with *two* fingers, i.e. a formulation that is a "mouth + finger + finger". What would that form look like? It is actually still only one finger but now it appears as if it is two, i.e., a "two finger" motion — one going "in" and one going "out" of a single mouth.[35] The sages are graphically describing a topological surface! The masters of concealment are ingeniously revealing the inner technology of a dual action "finger". This geometric configuration fits the description of the topological surface structure of the donut-like form known as a torus.

This is the last piece major piece of information missing from the Luz equation. We know the equation of the three cities that, all together, constitute one complete key. With the secret of the Luz bone we know the location of the keyhole. With the secret of "How did he show them" we know the "key's" mode of insertion. Now, we only need to know *how* to turn the key in order to begin to enter into the Kingdom of Luz.

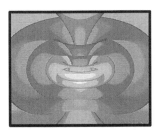

4. Turning the Key:
The Torah Torus

Although relatively new to its emerging role in the New Sciences a torus is a common form.[36] A bagel is torus shaped as is an inner tube and a doughnut.

Toroidal space is the area and volume of the doughnut-like shape of a torus. A major branch of geometry, that includes toroidal space, is the study of geometrical structures superimposed upon an area of curved space (known as a manifold). This special form has been used to describe a number of things in the theoretical and abstract realm as well as in the "real" world. (Einstein's theory of General Relativity describes the universe — the entirety of space and time — as a 4-Dimensional curved surface, i.e., a manifold.) Below are a few examples of some tori (plural for torus) and toroidal space:

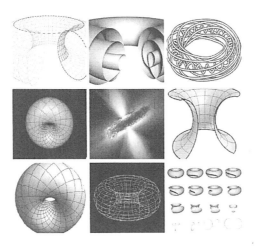

On the sub-micro atomic level the toroidal form is an important player in superstring physics[37] and, on the super-macro cosmological level scientists have suggested that the entire universe may, in fact, be shaped like a torus.[38]

> There is now a great deal of scientific and metaphysical information available to indicate that the Torus is the best model we have for attempting to understand the primal structure of the universe. What we are looking at is really the principal shape of consciousness itself being a spherical vortex of energy; a self-organizing and self-sustaining sphere of energy....[39]

From a Torah perspective this statement is simply a more scientific definition of the Talmudic Sage-Mystics' formulation of "God" or, more specifically, the Divine-human interface. Toroidal space is one of the most, if not *the* most critical model accessible now in our generation to begin to describe the relationship between Creator and creation, Divinity and humanity, soul and body and between higher and lower dimensionality. The toroidal movement of the torus is the secret to the Torah's well hidden method of "turning the key" within the Luz keyhole to enter into the Kingdom of Luz.

We must always bear in mind that a torus, like any of the scientific maps, models and metaphors bursting forth from the New Sciences in the Final Generation, is only a model and *not* what it is modeling, i.e., the sacred, esoteric truths of the Torah's *Ohr Ganuz*—the higher-dimensional Hidden Light.

The toroidal form figures heavily into what is known as the esoteric study of "sacred geometry". This is a "meta-science" that

reveals how shape and form is the primary underlying principle of manifestation.

Since ancient times, "seers" have observed that the human aura (the *tzelem* of the Kabbalah and its iterations) appears as a series of nested spherical torus formations. This concept reappears in similar fashion across a huge number of different cultures. As will be shown below, Torah/Kabbalah not only confirms this observation and belief, but takes it even further. The Torah Torus (together with the teachings of HuG — the *hasadim* and *gevurot*) is the very core of the inner tradition of the Talmudic Sage-Mystics and Jewish consciousness.

In Jerusalem of the Mind and the Foundation Stone we are not interested in a static, motionless "doughnut", but rather in a dynamic, moving torus. A moving or rotating torus is a doughnut-shaped vortex of energy which is constantly turning itself inside out just like a rotating smoke ring. The geometric shape used to describe the self-reflexive nature of consciousness is the torus. The toroidal movement is the self-organizing way consciousness is designed. The torus generates a vortex of energy which bends back along itself and re-enters itself. It is continuously flowing back into itself. Thus the energy of a torus is continually renewing itself, continually affecting itself.

An examination of the torus shows that its very construction forms energy funnels or vortexes. All tori create energy vortexes. Energy can funnel up or down through it; the rotating nature of a torus generates a flow of energy through the torus, depending upon the speed of rotation of the torus and the kind of torus it is. Additionally, these two vortices have polarity, i.e., positive and negative boundaries or terminals. Now, what is the *Torah* Torus?

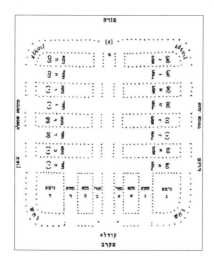

The diagram above in Hebrew and Aramaic is an original schema drawn by R. Shlomo Eliyashiv (known as the *Leshem*), the early 20th-century master kabbalist and chief expositor of the Kabbalah of the Gaon of Vilna.[40] It is a graphic description of his clarification of the Gaon of Vilna's commentary on a section from the *Zohar*. It is core to a field of highly advanced Zoharitic/Lurianic Kabbalah that is far beyond our purpose here. However, the archetypal design that it delineates is unmistakably and profoundly revelatory. This graphic depiction, based upon the Gaon's description, is virtually unknown even among Torah kabbalists, not to mention among academicians of comparative mysticism and popular "kabbalism". Yet, its implications are the final piece in the puzzle to the secret of how to "turn" the Luz key of the "mouth and the finger". This glyph contains a profound secret of the Talmudic Sage-Mystics — the Torah Torus.[41]

The diagram is mapping out the cosmic "circuits" of the higher dimensional "cranium/consciousness" of *Arich Anpin*, Supernal Man. (More specifically this "brain" is the aspect of the higher-dimensional "grandfather" as opposed to the aspect of the father, son, groom and husband. In simple theological language

Arich Anpin is the "Godhead"). This portrayal is an "aerial view", i.e., looking "down" at the top of the "head" with the bottom of the diagram being the back of the head ("west") and the top of the diagram is the face ("east"). The fundamental design is that of a central column diverging at its top into two branches that curve around to reunite at its original starting point. The Gaon of Vilna explains that this is the form of the singular cosmic serpent that reveals itself as "two" serpents only to reunite as one. These two serpents are also known as the two Leviathans.[42] In simple terms, the pattern of the Two-Tailed Leviathan is the primal structure of the never-beginning/never-ending ("never-not") dual-natured pulsating divine light (straight light and curved light) of the Ain Sof.

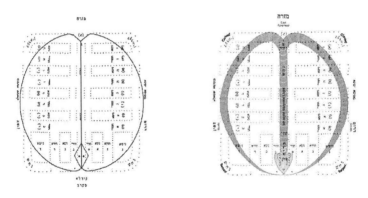

The diagram on the left is the identical one as above only that I have outlined the pattern defined in the original. The diagram on the right is also the original but now with my overlay of the two-tailed Leviathan clearly emphasizing the intended form (Although at this size they are not so legible, the English translations for the original Hebrew words are overlaid here as well.) This section of the Zohar (with the Gaon of Vilna's commentary and the *Leshem's* graphic depiction) is, with little question, the most unusual and mysterious form in the entirety of Torah literature. In fact, this strange form is the most unique shape in the annals of comparative religion, mysticism, mythology, alchemy and Jungian psychology. A serpent with its tail in its mouth is known as an uroboros and throughout these fields of study this universal motif is well known, studied and interpreted. This "Jewish" serpent, however, is unprecedented in that it is a serpent with *two* tails in its singular mouth! The Torah's Two-Tailed Uroboros is also "fractaling" (i.e., self-replicating fractured fractions of itself) in the mystery of the two Leviathans that are really one, as explained at length by the Gaon.[43]

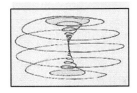

Now what does this flat 2-Dimensnional representation have to do with a 3-Dimensional spherical torus? It has everything to do with it because it is precisely *only* a 2-Dimensional representation of a 3-Dimensional spherical torus! When we geometrically project its flat surface unto a spherical surface, amazingly we have the Zohar's depiction of a dynamic, auto-rotating toroidal structure. The Two-Tailed Leviathan generates a vortex of energy which bends back along itself and re-enters itself. Continuously flowing back into itself, its "outside" becomes its "inside" and its "inside" becomes its "outside". (Utilizing the Möbius strip model its "outside" *is* its inside as, in reality, it is only one "side" with two surfaces.[44]) The Torah Torus is continually stimulating and energizing itself generating vortices at its "top" and "bottom". These two vortexes have polarity, i.e., positive and negative boundaries or terminals. Divine energy funnels up (and/or down) through it. A revolving torus is in a state of constant torque. This is due to the polarity of its two funnels at both ends.[45]

The dynamic rotating nature of a Torah torus creates an endless flow of divinity through its central column and all around itself.

The "serpentine" forms are simply describing the direction of the flow of these energies up and down through the central column (the "straight" Leviathan serpent) and then "turning back" on its own self (the "curved" Leviathan serpent). These pathways are the actual circuits being described in this section of the Zohar.

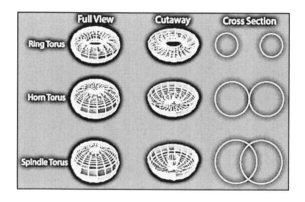

There are actually three types of standard tori as pictured above.[46] The ring torus is the true doughnut shape, i.e., with a hole or conduit through the middle. Pictured below is an example of a spindle torus where its own outer surface is being pulled and elongated up and down through its own self, i.e., it is not hollow but solid. Here it has been cut in half and opened up to see and experience it from the inside out.

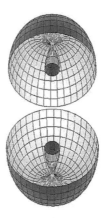

When a 3-Dimensional, spherical Two-Tailed Leviathan is superimposed onto this shape an astounding discovering is evident: This toroidal space is precisely the model that the Zohar, the Gaon of Vilna and the *Leshem* are describing. Moreover, Leviathanic toroidal space is not limited to the Zohar's specific subject of the cranial pathways of *Arich Anpin*. To the contrary, the higher-dimensional "cranial nerves" here being described are the fundamental formula for all patterns and configurations (*partzufim*) that proceed afterwards in the progression of the dimensional worlds, as is well known in Lurianic Kabbalah. The Leviathan torus is the root formula which then iterates and replicates itself throughout all existence, above and below.

This is the living tradition of the Talmudic Sage-Mystics who maintain that a constantly rotating toroidal form is what defines the mechanisms of consciousness itself — ours as well as that of the Divine Mind. According to the Kabbalah, all modes of consciousness and Torah based structures have a geometrical structure and all levels of reality are topological fields of tori within tori within tori! This is evident within the fundamental template of the Ten Sefirot and the Four Worlds model where it is axiomatic that "The end is rooted in the beginning". This is the kabbalistic formula of *"keter-malchut"* where the kingdom/*malchut* inverts on itself to become its own crown/*keter* and vise versa (as well as for the level above it and below it). This is also the well-known Shabbat liturgical verse, "Last in action [the bottom toroidal vortex], first in thought [the upper toroidal vortex]", i.e., the Shabbat — the seventh day of creation — funnels back up through its own "six days" of creation to reveal herself now as the "crown of creation".

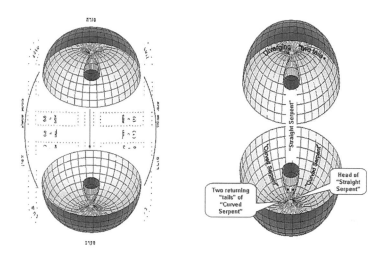

Thus far the Torah Torus. For our purposes here concerning the secret of how to turn the key to enter into the Kingdom of Luz, however, we are interested primarily in the toroidal entrance of the bottom contour that "funnels" a tunnel into the torus.

This is the Talmudic secret of the "mouth". As explained above, the dual movement of the "finger" is the secret of the act and movement of slowly and gently entering through the cave and into the tunnel that leads to Luz. This is the dynamic structure of a single finger movement "in" and "out". This is precisely the in and out dynamic of the funneling "to and fro" at the mouth and lip of the torus. This is the secret of "pushing" our 3D reality up against the 4D reality, back and forth, in order to create a subtle suction action. This is what stimulates the higher dimension portal to open up and receive the visitor into the City of Luz.

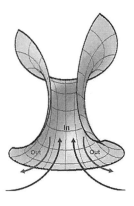

When this specific toroidal movement is mentally and experientially applied at the occipital cavity at a slight angle in the direction of the pineal center this is the aspect of the Canaanite "showing the House of Joseph the way in". This is also what the Maharal explains as to why it was spiritually necessary that the one who directed the Jewish scouts to the secret entrance of Luz had to specifically *not* be a Jew and also from the Canaanite nation. At that time the Canaanites represented the most corporeal and materialistic element of humanity. Yet, it was the very physicality and "fleshiness" of this Canaanite that was the missing component needed to "physically" push (and pull) from the *outside* of Luz in order to enter into the higher-dimensional *inside* of luz.[47] Below are six diagrams showing the progression from the original 2-

Dimensional drawing to the actual movement of "turning the key".

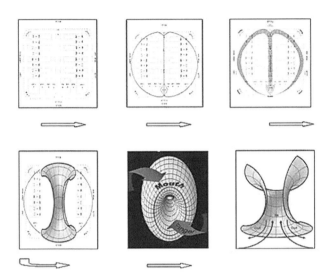

The objective of the inner mechanism of the "mouth and the finger" is to create an almost visceral sensation of the Canaanite's "toroidal suction" as explained. This is achieved by visualizing a constant self-revolving torus along a central axis, whether at an incline in the head running from the occiput to the hairline of the forehead or a straight axis running up and down the spine. When the central column of a torus (whether the "spine" is hollow like a ring torus or solid like a spindle torus) is dynamically turning its surface in on itself, the subtle toroidal suction and movement is generated.

Using the model of the Möbius strip, the inner concavity of the toroidal space from its inside, becomes from its outside, its own convexity — there being only "one side" with "two surfaces". This technique helps locate your own spinal vortex which then opens upinto the hidden 4th dimensional entrance to the Luz cave. By turning the three dimensional surface of our outer reality ("Flat-land") in on itself it now becomes the actual gate into a higher, but parallel and intersecting, higher-dimensional "sacred space". We are inverting our consciousness by using our three dimensional reality to move in a fourth direction "perpendicular" to our apparent reality. This is the four dimensional world of Luz that once you are "inside" there is no longer linear space, liner time or linear movement. Rather, every "moment" and "point" reveals itself to be a fractal of eternity — truth, consciousness and immortality precisely as the Talmudic Sage-Mystics described the other-worldly city of Kushta (Luz). The esoteric art of inverting one's physicality within one's own body is the very ladder of Jacob's vision that connected the "earth" with the "heaven" and upon which he entered into Beit El/Luz. The method of 'funneling a tunnel" through the sensate material world is turning the key to the new Jerusalem of the Mind — geographically in Israel and physically within one's own inner Jerusalem.

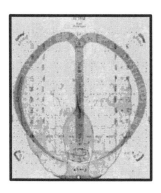

5. Luz Key Technology

Below is a review and additional techniques that can be used to help one enter into the Kingdom of Luz. The Torah Torus, as practitioners know, can be applied to anything and everything in life with truly amazing results and especially to the world of prayer and meditation. The same techniques and experiences can be applied to Luz, the only difference being that Luz and all of its iterations and rectifications (*tikunim*) now become the goal and destination point. For example, whereas the prayer torus is visualized encompassing the entire body and/or the entire universe, the Luz torus is applied specifically in the area of the occiput, at the atlas bone and around and in the pineal gland, i.e., the Luz cave entrance, the luz bone and the higher-dimensional Luz essence, *Mayim Chayim*, the Living Liquid. In other words, instead of the toroidal movement rotating around the spinal axis, the toroidal movement is now rotating around the cranial axis between the occiput and the pineal body (and/or at the hairline, the coordinate for the head *tefilin*, where the two "tails" of the Leviathan diverge from each other.

Here are the basic techniques for building a *Torah Torus* prayer canopy (*chupah*) which can then, as applicable, be applied in daily life, to prayer and/or to Jerusalem of the Mind and beyond.

1. Visualize your torus form surrounding you and then become the torus beginning with your spine as the elongated "hole" or shaft of light penetrating up through the center of the torus. Keep it elastic, e.g., make it as small as your pineal body or as large as the universal body. Keep your motor running (and your breath breathing) — animate your torus so it is perpetually revolving in and out on itself, through itself and within itself. Your torus is both you and more than you.

2. Maintain the torsion and the torque of the polarities between your negative and positive terminals, the base of your spine and the base of your head, your humanity and your divinity, this dimension and the higher dimension, your feminine stimulation and your masculine radiation, your feminine gynergy and your masculine spinergy, your imprisoned pain (and/ or of the world) and emotional compression and the redeemed joy and new spiritual expression.

3. Continually "feed" your needs and the needs of others into your lower vortex of the concaved funnel from below up through your central column and out though the Creator's convexed funnel of radiating Light. Feel it then radiating and showering down all around you to reunite with your lower vortex. Then repeat the Torus Prayer cycle again and again and again. Don't stop. This is the secret of true prayer. The fuel is the magnification and amplification of

your blood, sweat and tears. If you feed your needs into your torus furnace and fuel your fire and keep your torus moving, then your heat will become His heat, your needs will become His "needs" and you will have entered into the mystery of the Divine Flames of Love. If you feed your Torah Torus feedback loop enough times and with sufficient acceleration your prayers will be "heard" and simultaneously God's Own prayer will be answered — that you now know how to pray in the secret of Torah Torus prayer.

Here are basic techniques for more specific application to Jerusalem of the Mind, all the while staying in the sacred tension of your rotating toroidal space:

1) Imagine the Foundation Stone under the dome as a large iron bell that you are ringing with the clapper from the inside out. [48]

2) Imagine the Foundation Stone in Jerusalem as a giant "tuning fork". You strike it with your mind and it vibrates causing the resonance to vibrate your pineal body, and then back again.

3) According to reflexology and acupuncture, the upper part of each big toe corresponds to the pineal gland. Wiggle your big toes and then "draw" them up into the coccyx bone at the base of the spine as they merge into "one toe". Then bring it up to the spine and into the pineal gland. Now "wiggle" the big toe *inside* the pineal gland.

4) Anytime, anywhere, simply imagine you are inside the global Foundation Stone and the global Foundation Stone is inside your head. Again, in turn, your pineal is inside of the Temple Peniel and then the Temple Peniel is inside your pineal. Initially, this dynamic can appear like a hall of cascading mirror images, but the experience soon morphs into a nonlocalized feedback loop that has no distinct beginning or end. (Asking yourself rhetorically, "What came first, pineal or Peniel"? is also a Torah koan-like technique to quickly take you there.)

5) If truly "We want Mashiach, the Messiah, now"! then we have to be willing to envision what global messianic consciousness will be like. The obvious place to start is within one's own "personal globe", i.e., one's mind. We can stimulate the imminent flood of Adamic DMT by seeing it now within our own inner Jerusalem of the Mind. If one is not willing and desirous to begin experiencing one's own beginnings of higher consciousness then wanting it for all the Jewish people and the world are only empty words.

6) Close your eyes and immerse yourself in the inner darkness of your head. Now, find within the center of your brain your pineal gland and envision it as a pin point of bright white light. (Knowing the exact center of your head is not necessary because with practice your pineal gland will find its own center). Keep the pitch black dark-

ness as black as possible while forcing the pineal pin point to continually condense itself. Paradoxically, as the blackness becomes thicker and larger, in contrast the pin point of pineal light increases its luminosity. At first it may appear as a minute inner protrusion, then appearing with the brightness of a flashlight and finally with the radiance of a lighthouse directing its laser-like light in a full 360 degree radius. After practicing this technique for a period, then imagine taking your entire brain and cranium and sucking it all up into a very small opening, like the lip of a balloon, in the pineal light body. Your pineal will then be forced to become much bigger to accommodate the size of your head. But then, without losing the visual and kinetic sensation achieved so far, start over again by forcing the pin prick of pineal light to contract again into the minutest possible space. Then repeat this process again and again. This method will stimulate the pineal from the inside out and everything else will follow.

7) There are many more paths of entry into Luz and ways in which to stimulate the pineal gland. Here you can add your own techniques that you develop, either consciously or those that are revealed to you at the entrance to Luz from your own "inner Canaanite", who is there to show you the way.

Every pilgrim making the journey to Luz is unique as well as being at different stages in the journey. Therefore, everyone will experience the Kingdom of Luz somewhat differently from each other. A method that may work for one will not work for another. What worked with you yesterday may need to be revamped the next day. Colors, shapes, textures, sounds (and more) will morph and change. The edges of solidity become tessellated viscosity. The liquidity of one moment's experience becomes the surface topology for the next moment. As all practitioners have a t t e s t e d , as one enters deeper and deeper on the path the only constant in Luz is that one's Torah Torus, like a spiritual kaleidoscope, will never be the same twice. Yet each experience will become more and more familiar, with an increasing sense that "I have been here before and I know this *Place*."

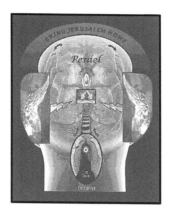

6. The P2P Keruvim HeadSet

This chapter introduces, to date, the most advanced applied P2P technology. It is predicated upon everything explained above in Part I and in Part II, including some of the techniques described there. This method is intended for the novice who has only an overview understanding of P2P, as well as for the advanced practitioner who, in one mode or another, has already entered into the city of Luz. This technology is based upon the utilization of the Ark of the Covenant and the two *Keruvim*, the male and female "cherubs" that sit atop its lid. The Ark of the Covenant and its inner connection to the Foundation Stone have been previously referred to (and are pictured in color on the front cover of this book). The actual mechanism of that connection will now be amplified.

Between the Two Keruvim

The Book of Exodus (25:10-22, 37:1-9) describes in detail this unusual structure which was the physical and spiritual center of the *Mishkan* (Tabernacle) continually throughout the period of the First Temple, King Solomon's sanctuary. The Divine Mind instructed Moses:

I will commune with you, and I will speak with you from above the ark-cover, *from between the two Keruvim,* which are on the Ark of Testimony.

Commenting on this verse the contemporary Torah and Kabbalah master Rabbi Aryeh Kaplan has written,[49]

...thus indicating that the primary influence of prophecy came though these two Cherubs in the Holy of Holies. What was true of Moses was true of the other prophets as well. During this time the Sanctuary, and later the First Temple, served as the focal point for all prophetic experience. The space between them was also seen as an opening into the spiritual dimension. In concentrating his thoughts between the Cherubs on the Ark a prophet was able to enter the prophetic state.[50]

A depiction of the Ark of the Covenant

The representation of these two winged creatures, one with the facial features of a male child and the other of a female child, is well known throughout the world (even with today's generation when the "Old Testament", outside of parochial schools, is almost no longer studied in school even as literature). Ironically, contemporary global knowledge of the Ark is due to Hollywood's influence, e.g.,

Indiana Jones and the Raiders of the Lost Ark. In this action-adventure film, the Ark of the Covenant plays the central role in the battle between the "good guys" and the "bad guys" due to its power to destroy one's enemies.[51]

The Ark of the Covenant destroying its enemies

Part I has made it clear that the centrality of the Foundation Stone in developing authentic Torah consciousness cannot be over emphasized. Likewise, the centrality of the Ark of the Covenant and its twin *keruvim* cannot be over emphasized. (We will use the Hebrew term *keruvim* and not "cherubs" or "cherubim" as these transliterations now have too many other connotations and associations).

In Part I the following Midrash was quoted:

> *As the navel is set in the center of the human body,*
> *so is the land of Israel the navel of the world...*
> *situated in the center of the world,*
> *and Jerusalem in the center of the land of Israel, and*
> *the Sanctuary in the center of Jerusalem, and the*
> *holy place in the center of the Sanctuary, and the*
> *Ark in the center of the holy place,*
> *and the* **Foundation Stone** *in the center of the holy*
> *place, because from it the world was founded.*

Imagine we are high above the world and are using a GPS (Global Positioning System) device in order to find the center, the root and the very essence of the Nation of Israel. First we are directed to the Land of Israel, then to Jerusalem and then to the Temple on Mt. Moriah. As we now zoom in on the Temple we are directed to the Holy of Holies and finally to the Ark of the Covenant resting upon the floor of the Foundation Stone. Our journey to the center of Israel, both the land and the people, is not fully complete, however, until we find our consciousness literally suspended between the figures of the twin *keruvim*. Behold, the vortex of space between the *keruvim* is the center of Torah consciousness! When the Ark was in existence and fully functioning, the center and foundation of Jewish consciousness emanated from this very point. Even the essence of the holy Torah emanates from this coordinate as attested to by the verse/formula (mentioned in the beginning of chapter 10), "For out of Zion [another code name for the Foundation Stone] will go forth Torah".

When we think about this artifact, it is a rather strange phenomenon. As known, there is a very strict Mosaic prohibition against making "molten images" — specifically images of heavenly entities. Yet, here is a molten gold statue of two angelic beings in the middle of the Holy of Holies — in the middle of Torah consciousness! In this case, it is an exception to the rule, as these molten images on the Ark were specially commanded by the Holy One, which overrides the general Biblical injunction.[52] We can appreciate that in order for this three dimensional image to be fashioned and placed in the center of the Temple, there must have been something very unique, very powerful and very necessary about it. What was the function of the Ark of the Covenant with its two *keruvim*? Moreover, just what are *keruvim*?!

Back to the Garden

Attempting to understand what these *keruvim* on the Ark are is apparently compounded by *another* set of *keruvim* that are often overlooked. This is in the Book of Genesis (3:26).

> And having driven out the *adam* [referring to both male and female] He stationed at the east of the Garden of Eden the *keruvim* and the flame of the ever-turning sword, to guard the way to the Tree of Life".

There are many explanations — psychological, spiritual, national and even ethical — of what these figures are and what they represent. Here we are not concerned with what either set of *keruvim* symbolize but rather *what do they do operationally*? But first, what are *keruvim*? They are higher-dimensional angelic entities. They are non-corporeal (except for the special set of *keruvim* of the Ark of the Covenant). Aside from the two primary sources just quoted, *keruvim* appear in the prophet Ezekiel's famous vision of the *Merkavah* — the Divine Chariot. They also appear in the prophet Isaiah's corresponding vision. Altogether, they appear over ninety times throughout Tanach. The difficulty in trying to define what they are is that they are very chameleon-like, appearing in different guises and in different roles. They can appear child-like as on the Ark and sword-wielding and protective as at the entrance to *Gan Eden*. They can be male or female, young or old. The image of the ox in Ezekiel's vision, several chapters later, morphs into a *keruv*, this time with the face of a mature man, and the Sages tell us, in a highly esoteric formula, that every night, "The Holy One rides upon His swift *keruv* and soars through 18,000 worlds".[53]

The mercurial nature of *keruvim* is apparent when we try to form a picture of the set of *keruvim* placed "East of Eden" (The first time *keruvim* are mentioned in the Torah). On the simple narrative level, they are defined variously as "Destroying angels"[54], "Terrifying apparitions"[55] or the "Angel of Death"[56]. The Midrash derives from the verse that "the flame of the ever-turning sword" is an aspect of the *keruvim* themselves as "They change ["ever-turning"]: sometimes they appear as men, sometimes as women, sometimes as spirits, sometimes as angles."[57] Moreover, their apparent role as ferocious guardians is only one aspect of their Edenic function. A Torah authority from the 19th century explains that, "Guarding the way to the Tree of life" can also be referring to the *keruvim's* role to *protect* and *preserve* the way so that the path will not be lost to mankind, so that we will be able to find the path again and make our way back from whence we have come! He supports this conclusion from the fact that the *Gan Eden* set of *keruvim* are fundamentally the same *keruvim* — the golden protectors — of the Ark of the Covenant![58] Thus, the *keruvim* know not only how to keep lower-dimensional curious seekers out but, like a semi-permeable membrane, they also know how to welcome true pilgrims in. The gates of Eden are also the path of return, the portal into higher-dimensional consciousness, the door into the Holy of Holies and the Foundation Stone. This is fundamental to the practice of Jerusalem of the Mind and this is the purpose of the P2P *Keruvim* HeadSet.

Again Rabbi Kaplan:

The *Cherubim* on the Ark in the Holy of Holies in the Temple were a focal point for the prophetic experience. These *Cherubim* in turn represented the *Cherubim* that guard the entrance to the "Tree of Life" in the Garden of Eden (Genesis 3:24). The "Tree of Life" corresponds to the *Sefirot* of *Atzilut* and refers to the highest spiritual experience that a prophet can attain. This confirms again that Ezekiel [in his visionary Merkavah experience] is trying to get into the Garden of Eden, into the prophetic state of Adam before the sin. As he begins to transcend the bonds that tie his mind and soul to the physical world, he is actually approaching the "Tree of Life". The first thing he encounters are its guardians, which are the *Cherubim*.[59]

The Torah is also referred to as a "Tree of Life" (Proverbs 3:18). This alludes to the fact that the mystery of prophecy is contained in the teachings of the Torah. It is for this reason that the *Cherubim* were placed on the Ark that contained the original Torah Scroll written by Moses. By concentrating on the space between these figures, the prophet could then obtain a vision and hear God's voice.[60]

The full nature of the *keruvim* is beyond the scope of the present work and requires a book unto its own (This would take us deep into the study of advanced Lurianic Kabbalah and Torah "angelology"). There is, however, one concept that will enable us to get a quick, yet deep grasp of an essential aspect of the nature of a *keruv*. By creating a play on the similarity in sound between the Hebrew word *keruv* and the English word "groove" we can gain a rather profound insight. A *keruv* is an inter-dimensional channel or "groove" permanently etched into the celestial terrain and the higher-dimensional Body of Adam. *Keruvim* function, not only as guardians *at* the gates, as in the case with *Gan Eden*, but they also function as the guides *within* the gates. The *keruvim* guide by morphing into a higher-dimensional train car or vehicle a *merkavah* — that the pilgrim "rides" along the *keruvim* tracks (Sometimes it can seem like an inter-dimensional rollercoaster!). *Keruvim* are the circuits and grooves of the tracks that direct and lead the one who has entered to the desired destination. *Keruvim* are the circuit boards of the Divine Mind. They are also similar to the multitude of tracks at a grand central railroad terminal that spoke off into various worlds and dimensions. Even the Holy One, Himself rides — as much as we can express that which we cannot the *keruv* grooves as it is written, "He [God] mounted a *keruv* and flew" (Psalms 18:11). This function of the *keruvim* is also explicit in the statement/formula of the Talmudic Sage-Mystics quoted above that, "The Holy One rides upon His swift *keruv* and soars through 18,000 worlds".[61]

Where can these *keruvim* take you? They can guide you to essentially everything that occurred at or is associated with the Place of the Foundation Stone. These destinations include fractal returns along the "Path of the Tree of Life", entering through the multi-tiered portal opened up by the Patriarch Jacob, teleporting to the inner most secret of the Foundation Stone, visiting the eternal city of Luz, also known as *Kushta* ("Truth") and more. A *keruv* is a groove in the Torah topology of the cosmic torus.[62] So, how does one get into a P2P "*keruv* groove"?

For the purpose of the P2P HeadSet we need only know this: the set of twin *keruvim* are a type of amplifying system and a stereophonic set of speakers. Due to their unique construction, their role in the Temple service and where they are rooted in higher-dimensional reality, they have the ability to stimulate and magnify the spatial coordinate where they are resting. What do they amplify? During the many centuries when they were operational they amplified what was in the Ark upon which they rested: The broken fragments of the *original* set of Ten Commandments, the complete second set of the Ten Commandments and first Torah scroll that Moses personally wrote, dictated to him by the Creator.[63]

The *keruvim* also stimulate and amplify the *space* between each other, a most sacred place surrounded and protected by their overarching wings, which touch one another. This is due to the field of energy they produce. The fact that they are both male and female is very significant. As known in the Kabbalah, the "masculine" and "feminine" essence of the two *keruvim* contain within them literally every aspect of "masculine" and "feminine" throughout the entire universe, both physical and spiritual. This dual nature includes the *Ain Sof* and the *Light of the Ain Sof*, the Creator and creation, the Holy One and the *Shechinah*, God and His beloved Israel, *Metatron* and *Sandalphone*, straight, expanding light and curved, returning light, *hasadim* and *gevurot* (HuG), the male and female *Leviathan*, the "Next World" and "This World", the Twin Messiahs, heaven and earth, and on and on. There is a virtual endless array of these self-similar iterations that fractal up and down the inter-dimensional spectrum of existence and their essences are all contained in the two *keruvim* of the Ark of the Covenant! (As known, the purpose and function of this infinite array of polarities is not in and of for themselves, but rather all these "dualities" that are personified in the *keruvim* are only being utilized to generate and reveal a "new middle" (the *da'at*), i.e., the point singularity of absolute unification. This is the *tikun* of returning the branches of the Tree of Knowledge (of dualities) back into its root in the singular Tree of Life).

Male and female are also positive and negative polarities. These two polarities create two terminals. These two terminals create a type of "battery" that, when charged and "turned on", like a spark plug, generate a current between them. This field of energy, in turn, opens up a vortex. The structure of this field is not random. Rather it moves in a toroidal fashion, as explained above where the Torah Torus was introduced. Yes, as well as the space surrounding the ark is toroidal, the spatial topology *between* the *keruvim* is also a Torah Torus! Now, while "holding" the toroidal vortex in your mind's eye, there is one more living image that must be integrated into the *keruvim* in order for the Gate of the Heavens, the door to *Beit El*-the House of God to open up and receive those who desire to enter. This is the set of *keruvim* from the Book of Genesis. When we superimpose the twin *keruvim* from *Gan Eden* – also a polarity of "male" and "female" — onto

147

the set from the Ark, the vortex generated reveals itself as none other than the return to "the path to the Tree of Life".

At this stage one does not need to have any specific image of the *Gan Eden keruvim*. Only a sense or spiritual intuition of what these *keruvim* are is required. Minimally, unlike the golden *keruvim*, these *keruvim* are not metallic. They contain living, organic elements within them. Here the "revolving sword" alludes to the essences of the five senses — smell, sound, vision, taste and touch. Any one or more of these "human" aspects, when superimposed upon the golden, metallic *keruvim* is more than enough to open the vortex to the higher-dimensional *Gan Eden*. For example, one can imagine the aroma from Eden wafting towards you and now emanating from the golden *keruvim*. (In fact, the sacred Temple incense was offered in front of Ark of the Covenant on Yom Kippur by the Kohen Gadol. One can also experience one's consciousness, together with the *keruvim*, being enveloped by the thick cloud of protective smoke[64]).

The Arc of Conquering Love

Aside from its pivotal role in the sacred Temple service, its ability to destroy its enemies and its role in prophecy, the Ark of the Covenant performed another function, one that lies at its very heart. The *keruvim*, as explained, are creatures molten from gold with large wings each with the face of a child, one male and one female. We should not think, however, that because they were in the likeness of children they did not also have a mature, sensuous and deeply loving adult-to-adult relationship. Why then are these *keruvim* depicted as children? The truth is that there is another set of *keruvim* and they do, in fact, have the faces and behavior of mature adults! The Talmudic Sage-Mystics are very clear concerning this other mode of *keruvim* when they delineate between a *keruv* with a "small face" (*appay zutra*), i.e., the face of a child and a *keruv* with a "large face" (*appay ravrevay*), i.e., the face of an adult.[65] It is this "physical", in addition to spiritual love, between the mature *keruvim* that reflects the eternal, divine love between the Holy One and the people of Israel!

> When the children of Israel would ascend to the Temple on the festivals the *Kohanim* would role up the curtain [partitioning off the Holy of Holies] for them and show them the *keruvim* which were clinging to one another in embrace and the *Kohanim* would tell them, "Behold, your fondness before the Omnipresent (*Makom*) is like the fondness between a man and a woman".[65]

This description, together with a number of other metaphors that the Sages use to describe the Ark and its *keruvim*, are referring to the deepest soul and heart-based love throughout all existence. The interpenetrating love between the adult *keruvim* is an iterating microcosm of the ever-increasing, rapturous desire found in King Solomon's Song of Songs — the most spiritually romantic book of the holy Torah. The Sages actually use verses and their motifs from the Song of Songs to reflect the degree of ecstatic love embodied between the *keruvim*.

But where are the outer forms of the adult *keruvim*? We only see the child-like faces of these winged entities. Rather, the heart of the

Ark is a well-kept secret. Only when one enters into the winged, canopied space between the "lower", young *keruvim,* do they reveal their nature also as the "higher" older *keruvim.*[66] Astoundingly, the young *keruvim* are the gate (the "grooves") that opens into a passage way that reveals the older *keruvim* at the other end! (For the one who understands these adult *keruvim* are none other than iterations of the *keruvim* of *Gan Eden.*)

There is much more to the secret life of *keruvim,* but for our purposes the essential point is clear. As one enters into the mystery of the *keruvim,* the vortex that opens up between them is also a "Star-Gate" from which emanates unparalleled, higher-dimensional cosmic love. It is this infinite source of divine love that lies at the heart of the Ark of the Covenant. And it is this divine "arc" of electrifying love pulsating between them that can also be generated with the P2P *Keruvim* HeadSet. This arc of love is so powerful it can defeat our enemies simply by penetrating them with rays of messianic light that emanate out of the pineal center in our heads, while simultaneously emanating out of the *Even Shetiya!* This is conquering love. It conquers and is victorious not through the destruction of those who wish to destroy us, but rather — after burning away the membrane or residue of *klipah* — it extracts the fractal sparks of holiness and, in effect, transforms the very evil itself.[67]

The arc of love being generated by the Ark of the Covenant is not only the quintessential love between man and woman, but it is also the love the Creator has for all humanity, all life and all existence. It is with the power of this love — the very heart of the *keruvim* — that has the ability to stimulate and "wake up" the dormant *Even Shetiya,* both one's personal pineal Foundation Stone from within and the global Peniel Foundation Stone from without. As explained at the end of Chapter 3 Part I, the *klipah*/shell the golden Dome of the Rock — that currently surrounds and imprisons the global Adamic pineal gland need not be removed through external force from the outside. Rather, with the power of our consciousness, amplified and directed with the technology of the P2P *Keruvim* HeadSet, we can melt down the gilded dome, reconstitute it and morph it into the very golden *keruvim* themselves! It is this love that is also referred to in the words of the prophet, "And it will be in the end of days, I will pour out My *ruach*/spirit upon all flesh, and your sons and daughters shall prophesize; your elders shall dream dreams, your young men shall see visions".[68] This *ruach*/spirit is the Living Liquid of God's love, the higher-dimensional, universal M-DMT — Messianic consciousness dripping with *Ohr Ganuzic* Light (*Ohr Ganuz* = The Hidden Light).

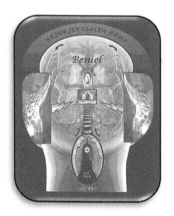

Putting on the HeadSet

The P2P *Keruvim* HeadSet requires meditating on the above graphic and visualizing it within your head. The accompanying black and white graphic of the HeadSet is found in color on the back of the book. If possible one should print out a full page color copy (best on glossy or photo paper) and regularly concentrate on it to the point where it is kinesthetically, if not viscerally, experienced within one's own head.[69] The P2P *Keruvim* HeadSet is designed to be a form of internal VR – virtual reality. To make it work it must be 99% experiential and subjective. The remaining one percent of your objective thinking is there only to keep you directed and in alignment with the details of the "map". Any thinking and analysis of the components, i.e., the information in Part I and in Part II, is now left behind. As you wear the HeadSet you *become* the HeadSet. You are Jerusalem of the Mind.

There are many paths of entry that lead to the New Jerusalem and each one will find his or her "quick induction" method. One can always begin — anytime and anywhere — by rhetorically asking one's self the question, "Where is my center?" or "Where is my true home"? There are endless paths and spiritual highways where the P2P HeadSet will take you. Use only what works for you and customize your HeadSet to fit your consciousness.

The following is a general summary of the methodology for "putting on" the P2P *Keruvim* HeadSet:

Look into the graphic. Gaze at the images of the two golden *keruvim* that you can find on the Internet or simply concentrate on the picture that is on the front or back cover of this book. Then project the image to the very center of your brain with your pineal gland in the middle between the two polarized *keruvim*. Now, project your consciousness into the Holy of Holies in the Temple in Jerusalem, again visualizing *your* pineal energy suspended as an orb of glowing toroidal energy (or whatever you may experience) between the *keruvim*. Then return to your personal inner Ark of the Covenant within your cranium. Continue oscillating back and forth between your pineal Foundation Stone and the *Peniel* Foundation Stone generating an "arc" of sacred energy that is "looped", like the infinity sign, into itself. With practice this method will open up a vortex between the molten figures centered in your pineal body. The pineal/Foundation Stone contains the essence and the sound of the Living Liquid and the *keruvim* are the amplifiers and speakers. Now (or at any stage), within the space of your revolving toroidal vortex, repeat or think "Bring Jerusalem Home". You are making a pilgrimage to your inner city of the New Jerusalem, while simultaneously making a pilgrimage to the outer city of the New Jerusalem. Both paths take you home and "There is no place like home". Plug in, Turn it on and "Bring Jerusalem Home".

The following is a detailed step-by-step process intended especially for, but not limited to, beginners.

Ten Steps to P2P Consciousness

1. Close your eyes and, *without yet entering your head*, visualize or sense a point in the center of your cranium. This middle point is also aligned along an east-west axis that runs at an angle from the occiput at the lower back of the head to the top of the forehead at the hairline. (As explained in Part I Chapter 9, one's face is always "east" with the back always being one's "west").

2. Take a deep inhalation and draw the energy up from the bottom of your feet, through your spine and up to the base of your head into the area of the occiput. (If sitting, the breath can begin at the base of the spine). Also, as explained in Part II Chapter 5, with this step you can bring up through your spine/central column any elements of negativity, anxiety, pain and *klipot*/shells as they will natural-ly be flushed out and purified as you enter the Luz cave.

3.　With a finger or thumb lightly separate your hair (the "foliage" of the "Luz tree") at the back of the head covering the occiput and press once firmly at the indentation immediately below the occipital ridge. (This is the switch" with which to open up the HeadSet and it is also based upon the secret of the "mouth" and the "finger" explained in Part II Chapter 9. For the experienced practitioner this step may develop naturally and will not be necessary).

4.　From your position at the occipital "cave" opening, slowly release the breath in the exhalation and visualize the air blowing into your head, as through a rotating smoke ring. Along the central east-west (front-back) axis you are creating a corridor or central column of an elongated self-revolving torus. (In the Headset graphic the toroidal movement is indicated by the four arrows). You are *not* yet inside your head. Rather, you are preparing to enter into your sacred toroidal space. When you enter, the activated toroidal movement will be the "ground" upon which all your consciousness takes place. With practice the toroidal movement and toroidal consciousness becomes second nature. You only have to notice and acknowledge the toroidal space. (The secret of the Torah Torus is explained in Part II Chapter 4).

5.　With your thought, enter into the dark Luz cave and remain just inside the entrance. (The Luz cave is explained in Part II Chapter 1.)

6.   Through the initial darkness of the cave distinguish a pin-point of the most powerful light imaginable at the end of the 45° toroidal tunnel ascending 49 stairs, rungs or ribs in the corridor. (The specific number 49 is not necessary. It could be any value you chose or none at all. Units of 49 simply convey a longer distance — generating more polarity — from the beginning of the tunnel to your inner sanctum).[70] Note that you are *not* yet inside the Place from where the light is emanating. You only are peering at it from a distance, but your energy and heightened sense of expectation is building up, as if you are saying to yourself "What could be the source of that super intense, sacred other-worldly light"!? Prepare now to enter your Inner Temple of the Holy of Holies in the very center of your pineal gland.

7.   Now in one fell swoop, as if a video camera immediately zooms in on an extreme close-up of the *keruvim*, your consciousness, like an orb of pulsating light, becomes the very point between them. *Your pineal/Peniel center is the source of the higher-dimensional light!* Your pineal gland occupies the exact coordinate of the vortex that is now opening up between the two *keruvim*. You shoot up from the cave/tunnel to the space between the *keruvim* as if you were instantly teleported there. You are in your Inner Temple, radiating with unimaginable holiness and hermitically sealed off from any and all external thoughts and forces[71].

8. Put on and wear the two *keruvim* as if they were earphones. Maintain the two *keruvim*, as if they are speakers on the right and left of your pineal vortex. Keep the energy/waves from the two speakers balanced and stay firmly plugged into the "socket" of your pineal port. (To help focus your concentration you can use your two ears or the two hemispheres of the brain to represent the two *keruvim*).

9. Now turn up the volume of your P2P *Keruvim* HeadSet by using the password, *"Bring Jerusalem Home!"* or simply *"Yerushalayim"*.

10. See the *Mayim Chayim*/Living Liquid of your personal *Even Shetiya* as it begins to drip and bathe you with its higher-dimensional anointing oil. Now, take your entire experience into the collective *Even Shetiya* in Jerusalem and witness its *Mayim Chayim*/Living Liquid drip and stream through your pineal and out to the world. If desired, you may now (or at any time) bring your heart and all the positive feelings of prophetic global love associated with it, as explained above, into your pineal temple and vice versa.

You can use all of the steps above or any of the steps in any order that works for you. Or you can create your own with the components. The P2P HeadSet (as with all the P2P techniques) is modular, i.e., you can take any of the components and the order of entry and move them and combine them as you wish.

Here is a short version:

- Focus on inhaling from the feet (or base of spine) up to the occiput.
- Focus on exhaling from the occiput to the pineal gland.
- Focus on centering your pineal between the two *keruvim.*
- Focus on "Bring Jerusalem Home" or simply "*Yerushalayim.*"

Here is the essence:

Envision your consciousness inside the pineal center of your head and, while envisioning the golden *keruvim* and meditating on Jerusalem, steadily hold your consciousness there between the *keruvim.*

Whether you are going through all ten steps, or using the short version or simply following the path of your own intuition, contextually it is important to remember this: Know that you are constructing a "docking station" for messianic consciousness and you are specifically doing so by uniting modern scientific discovery with ancient esoteric Jewish wisdom. This act of synergistic unification alone is a sign of imminent global transformation. Practicing P2P, in and of itself, is helping to stimulate and reveal the incoming messianic light.

Study and review Part I and Part II of this book, practice daily as much as possible and customize the system to the specific contours of your heart, mind and soul. Little by little, subtlety (or not), M-DMT will begin to be generated. Anyone can share in this experience and divine service, whether or not you have experienced exogenous DMT, ayahuasca or a non-ordinary state of consciousness. "You only have to convince your brain that you have done this, and it will then deliver this staggering altered state".[72]

If the techniques activating P2P consciousness mentioned in the previous chapters are compared to different types of automobiles, then the P2P *Keruvim* HeadSet would be a rocket ship. If seriously used on a regular basis, in comparison to a rocket ship, the HeadSet would be the Starship Enterprise switching into warp-speed. As this particular method consists only of a few components and a few steps, its technology is so simple that a beginner with only a minimal knowledge of the workings of Jerusalem of the Mind can use it with impressive results. Yet, it is so powerful that a more advanced practitioner can use it to begin to generate endogenous M-DMT. This is one of the most powerful — and ancient — ways to open up the P2P circuit, certainly when turbocharged with the topological mechanics of the Torah Torus.

The following was written a professional therapist who studied with me over a period of time and has been utilizing P2P and Luz technology for several years now. He has taken many clients, individually and in groups, on hour or longer "Luz cruises" where the whole process is directed and takes place while laying flat on the back. The following is the format he uses with participants while they are standing or sitting. In this application it begins straight away with putting on the HeadSet.

P2P Directions (2nd Set)

1. Put on your P2P Keruvim HeadSet.

2. While doing holotropic breathing (rapid chest breathing through the nose), create a laser-like line from your occipital area, through the pineal, to

the top of the forehead. Then bring it back to the occipital area across both ears. Do this for about 20 minutes.

3.   Imagine putting your hand down through your spine and bring up any emotion, feelings, or intentions back up to the occipital area.

4.   Now begin penetrating the occipital area until you either see the pinprick white light or the landscape changing colors. Once that occurs, go up at a 45 degree angle into your pineal gland.

5.   When in your pineal, create a toroidal field from your feet (or base of the spine) to the top of your head then back to the feet. Do this for about 5 minutes.

6.   Now it is time to do the P2P toroidal field from your pineal to your Foundation Stone, then back to the pineal, then back to your Foundation Stone, etc. This will generate resonance with the global Foundation Stone which is the most powerful energy vortex on the planet. Do this for about 5 minutes.

7.   Lastly, bi-locate (project) yourself into the Foundation Stone again creating the large toroidal field from the feet (or base of spine) up to your head, and then back to the feet. At some point you will know when to slow the torus down and just experience what comes to you — feelings, thoughts or images.

Throughout the day you will need to penetrate the occipital area again to gain access into the pineal gland. At some point this will no longer be necessary because you will *be* in the pineal.

M-DMT and the Return of Prophecy

The essential mechanics of the P2P *Keruvim* HeadSet, i.e., of projecting one's mind between the two *keruvim*, appear to be one of the methods, possibly even prerequisite, as to how the prophets stimulated their own endogenous higher states of consciousness. This premise is also based upon the hypothesis that, in one form or another, endogenous DMT (and/or other endogenously generated neuro-chemical agents) plays a requisite role in the prophetic experience, together with the various modes of *ruach haKodesh* ("divine transmission", lit. holy spirit). Note that the only new element that is being added (*chidush haTorah*) is that we are using our *own* pineal gland to center our consciousness. The most ancient of Jewish traditions is being reunited with a discovery from the cutting edge of science. This confluence alone is revelatory, prophetic and truly messianic. (This is explained at length in Part I.)

The premise that endogenous DMT is the medium through which prophetic consciousness manifested should not surprise us. It is well known in Torah that "miracles" do not appear "miraculously" out of nowhere. Rather, in order for any aspect of a higher-dimensional interpenetrating reality — the heavenly "next world" — to interface with any aspect of our lower-dimensional reality — the earthly "this world" reality — requires a "docking station" for the higher-dimension to "land" here. This is true even if the lower dimensional "docking station" is only the smallest artifact or minute amount of substance. There are myriad examples of this, both in Scripture and in the episodes in the lives of the Talmudic Sage-Mystics.

A classic example of this phenomenon is the festival of

Chanukah. It was a "miracle" that from one cruse of oil there was sufficient oil to burn for eight days. Yet, the miracle still required an element of the lower reality through which it could manifest. The single cruse of oil, aside from its own role as one of the eight days, was also the medium though which the other seven days could reveal themselves. Likewise, a similar phenomenon is being supplied by the molecular nature of the DMT that then allows the spirit or "soul" of DMT to clothe itself within the "body" of DMT. As to what comes first, the visionary consciousness descending from above clothing itself in the DMT or the DMT being chemically stimulated from below which then "draws down" the M-DMT is a question. The answer, however, may not be simply "this" or "that", but like the proverbial "chicken and the egg" both are occurring *co-terminus* as they are innately looped into one another.

It is fundamental to a Torah based cosmology that the state of consciousness known as prophecy will return to the Nation of Israel, as well as to the rectified Nations of the World. This is generally considered to be vouchsafed for the Messianic Era. There are, however, Torah authorities, including Maimonides, who maintain that the phenomenon of prophecy will return *before* the advent of the Messiah.[73] As explained above in Part I Chapter 5 The River of Light: Global DMT, this necessary rebirth of prophecy will be the beginning of the fulfillment of the prophet Joel (3:1), "And it will be in the end of days, I will pour out My *ruach*/spirit upon all flesh, and your sons and daughters shall prophesize; your elders shall dream dreams, your young men shall see visions".[74] As explained in Part I, this *ruach*/spirit is the Living Liquid, the M-DMT — the higher-dimensional root of physiological DMT.

At these times, the relationship between prophecy and DMT is hypothetical and controversial. But there appears to be more than a reasonable assumption that the practice of P2P, especially when the model of the *keruvim* is integrated, may play a direct role in the prophesied return of prophecy. As known regarding prophecy, there are many levels and gradations. *Ruach HaKodesh* itself is one of these levels and it, in turn, has its own levels and gradations (as reflected in the verse from the prophet Joel quoted above).

The most important principle to bear in mind is this: Through the daily "wearing" of the P2P *Keruvim* HeadSet, one is creating a "station" for many of the elements of global messianic consciousness to "dock". Actively working Jerusalem of the Mind is actively building a "docking station". The realm of higher-dimensional reality needs us as much and even *more* than we need it, as the Sages teach, "More than the calf need to suckle the mother cow needs to nurse".[75] Truly, Adam's original higher-dimensional consciousness is desperately longing to land. It needs our vessels for its *Ohr Ganuz* to reveal itself.

From a multi-dimensional perspective, the Messianic Era and beyond (e.g., *Olam HaBah*) is already here — not metaphorically, not poetically and not as part of a religious "wish list". It is *literally* here now. In the words of the Talmudic Sage-Mystics, *Olam HaBah* is the "World that has *already* come". And it keeps coming and coming and coming. It is a corresponding, free-standing interpenetrating dimension in which our 3D reality is embedded. It is the hidden fourth direction, the missing fourth coordinate and the collapsed fourth field of reality. We should not expect the Messiah to only appear to us from the "heavens", i.e., from *outside* of us. What we are looking for — consciously or not — is also *inside* of us. As explained above, miracles are not a divine form of stage magic. "Heaven", i.e., higher-dimensional realities, in order to reveal themselves to us, need a minimal point — even something as small as a pineal gland (the size of a grain of rice) from which to begin to manifest.

The pineal body may very well be that little landing pad and it is through its release of earthly DMT/M-DMT, that it could be the very advent of the messianic return of prophecy, now in our generation. We are referred to as the Final Generation because we are the end of the line, the end of time as we know it. We — our bodies, minds and souls — are teetering on the edge of time and space. What we refer to as the "messianic future" is simply higher- dimensional reality made manifest in a lower dimension. And that future is now. "And the one who understands will understand".

Endnotes
Part II

1   Part II is essentially intended for intermediate and advanced P2P Practitioners, Luz meditators and Torus prayer practitioners who are familiar with Part I. Additionally, viewing both DVD documentaries, *The Burdensome Stone* and *The Spirit Molecule*, is recommended. Although Part II continues the detailed exploration of Part I, it is still only an introduction to this vast subject. Many as yet unopened "hyperlinks" exist and therefore, as the Talmudic Sage-Mystics state, "one must compare one thing to another" and "the one who understands will understand".

2   The Gaon of Vilna wrote (*Even Shleimah*, p. 42), "The Aggadot on the surface appear as wasted expressions, God forbid, yet within them are concealed all the secrets. This is alluded to in the verse, "And he is afflicted because of our sins" (Isaiah 53:5). This passage ["Behold, my servant will prosper... And he is afflicted because of our sins..."] is referring to Moses. The intention is that due to the sin of the Bitter Waters (*May Mareeva*) it was decreed upon Moses that the Torah of Moses (*Torat Moshe*) — his holy teachings — would be desecrated by being clothed in forms such as these [superficially strange Aggadic tales] which have given a place for the scoffers in each generation to belittle them. This is what Moses petitioned from God: not to conceal the secrets of the Torah in these forms, but it was not granted to him. This is the matter of Moses' death and his burial outside of the Land of Israel. In the future the secrets within them will be revealed and this is the New Torah that will be revealed in the future".

A major expounder of the Gaon of Vilna, R. Shlomo Eliyashiv, the *Leshem* wrote (*Leshem Shevo veAchlama, Sefer Day'ah, D'rush Etz haDa'at*, end), "... there are numerous Aggadot of the Sages which are difficult even to listen to and one's sensibilities are astonished at them. Yet, within them are hidden the secrets of the Torah. This is all due to the emanations of the Light of Knowledge becoming clothed in the *klipot*/shells and in the external forces, God save us. The exile of the Shechinah, the exile of the People of Israel and the exile of the Torah are all due to the original fall of Adam".

3   Tractate *Sotah* 46b.

4   Luz has also been translated as an almond tree (see e.g., Tosafot, *Berchorot* 8a, s.v. *Tarnegolet* arguing for luz to be almond against Rashi (and others) who translate luz as hazelnut). In the context of the rabbinical secret of Luz, however, hazelnut appears more applicable. First off, there is another specific Hebrew term for almond which is *shakade* and it is used elsewhere in Scripture. (The Modern Hebrew word for an almond tree is *shekaydiya*). Moreover, an ancient Midrash states that one of the reasons the city was called Luz was because, like the luz nut, it was completely sealed on all sides. This description fits a hazelnut, which is almost spherical with no indentations or edges. This is not the case with an almond. Esoterically, the Ramchal School (R. Moshe Chayim Valle, Judges, *loc. cit.*) explains that "The entrance was specifically concealed beneath a luz tree whose fruit is hidden and sealed within its shell. This alludes to the aspect of *yesod*, containing both masculine and feminine in a hermetically protected union. A walnut [for example], alludes to the aspect of *malchut* which is divided into separate sections". Although, the distinction is made there between a luz nut and a walnut (and not specially an almond), it is evident that his depiction of the luz nut fits our hazelnut and not an almond.

Additionally, within this context, it is pointed out *(ibid.)* that the tribe of Joseph is also the aspect of *yesod*, as is known, and the city of Luz is the *yesod* of the Land of Israel. The Zohar informs us that, in terms of the twenty-two letters of the Hebrew alphabet, the letter "*tet*" is the "soul root" of the City of Luz. This letter, as is known, is also associated with *yesod* as the Zohar again states concerning the quality of *yesod*, "[The ultimate] Good is hidden within it ["*tet*"= yesod]". Therefore, the entrance to the city was hidden and concealed *(ibid).*

The actual term used here for the entrance to the city of Luz is "*mevo ha-*

ir" which is the only instance throughout Tanach where these two words are used together (*mavo* by itself and together with other words appear numerous times in Tanach). *Mevo* more correctly translates as "the way into the city" or "the approach to the city", the root being *b-v-a*, meaning "to come", i.e., "going and coming", interaction and intercourse. *Mavo*, and a common term for intimate intercourse — "*biah*" — are derived from the same root. (*Metzudat David*, loc. cit.). Following the equation just established, that the tribe of Joseph, the City of Luz, and the Luz nut are all iterations of *yesod* energy, the somewhat unique usage here of the term "*mevo ha-ir*" is apparent. The text uses it specifically as it is alluding to the secret mode and technique of entering through the foliage of the Luz tree (discussed below), the hollow in the trunk and the cave that leads into the extra-dimensional City of Luz.

5   Talmud *Sotah* 46b, *Sukkah* 53a, *Tanna D'Vei Eliyahu Zuta* Chapter 16.

6   Talmud *Sanhedrin* 97a.

7   "*Eleh, zekenim sh'bah, biz'man sh'Da'atan katza alayhem*", lit. "Rather, the elderly there, when their minds became weary". The term used to refer to their "minds" is *da'at*, the "middle brain", which alludes to the pineal body (upper *da'at*) as well as the occiput, cerebellum, corpus callosum and atlas vertebra (lower *da'at*) as explained further in the main text below. This is another code word the sages are using to allude to the fact that everything about Luz concerns the secret of the physiological and higher-dimensional *da'at* and how to access it.

8   Although Jerusalem was in the territory of Benjamin, a narrow finger of the tribe of Judah extended unto the Temple Mount. The boundary between the two (Judah from Leah and Joseph's brother Benjamin from Rachel) met at the altar (*Megilah* 26a).

9   There is an additional significance to Jacob's city of Luz that actually lies at the bedrock of the scientific research concerning the pineal gland and its relationship to Peniel — the P2P equation. Regarding the significance of Jacob's "ladder", the Gaon of Vilna has stated, "It is impossible to climb a ladder whose top reaches towards the heavens without first stepping on the

rungs of the ladder that are stationed near the earth. This is the essential idea that was conveyed to our father Jacob in his vision of the ladder." (Quoted by his disciple R' Hillel of Shklov in *Kol HaTor, Sha'ar Be'er Sheva*, near the end of section 10.) The full context of this quote is found in *The Secret Doctrine of the Gaon of Vilna*, Volume I, p. 146. In other words, by analogy it is impossible to grasp the full implications of spiritual truth without understanding its relationship to scientific fact.

10   *Chidushei Aggadot Maharal miPrague*, Tractate *Sotah*, 46b. He writes further:

Rashi z"l explained that these attributes [i.e., impervious to death, never destroyed, etc.] are referring to the Luz that the Canaanite built. It is clear, however, that the intention of the Talmud is as we have said [earlier in his commentary] that it is specifically referring to Jacob's Luz, as it is implicit in the Midrash Rabba *parashat VaYeitzey*. Thus it appears. It is possible, however, to say that the city the Canaanite built, calling its name Luz, also had these attributes that were in Jacob's Luz.

The support the Maharal brings from the Midrash is questioned by some of the commentaries. They assert that the unique qualities of the Canaanite's second city of Luz (2) are out of place here in the Midrash Rabba *parashat VaYeitzey*. Rather, they explain that it was accidentally inserted there due to the similarity in name to Jacob's Luz, but they are, in fact, two distinct cities of Luz (0 and 2). Although acknowledging that there could also have been a separate and distinct foreign city of Luz, the Maharal emphasizes that the miraculous qualities of Luz are first and foremost associated with the higher-dimensional nature of Jacob's Luz (0) and thus the Foundation Stone and Jerusalem of the Mind.

11   The apparent obvious contradiction, however, can be avoided as the Maharal himself suggests that, "It is possible, however, to say that the city the Canaanite built, calling its name Luz, also had these attributes that were in Jacob's Luz". This begs the question, however, that if the second Luz (2) is, in truth, Jacob's Luz (0), then why does the verse inform us that it was a different Luz built in a foreign land? I answer this in the next paragraph of the text.

12   It is intriguing to note that the ancient capital of Tibet to this day is called

Lasa (or Lhasa). The second time Jacob returns to Luz in the Torah it is written "Luza" (lit. meaning towards Luz but also alluding to a feminine counterpart to the first Luz, as Luza would be the feminine form of the masculine Luz). From this perspective, i.e., the possible correlation between Luza and Lasa, it is interesting to note that the Samaritan Pentateuch (as well as two versions of their Targum) on Genesis 28:19 have Luza instead of Luz of our Masoretic text, i.e., the traditionally accepted Bible text.

It is noteworthy that another intriguing connection to Luz is found in the novel Lost Horizon (1933) by James Hilton. In 1937 the book was made into a timeless movie classic — Lost Horizon (Directed by Frank Capra, staring Ronald Colman, Jane Wyatt and John Howard). Shangri-La is a fictional land depicted in which five people stumble upon a hidden valley in the Tibetan Himalayas called Shangri-La where peace abounds and time has virtually stopped. Since the book and the movie, the term Shangri-la has come to denote a remote beautiful place where life approaches perfection, where truth reigns supreme and people dwell together in eternal peace.

The Shangri-La of Lost Horizon bears uncanny similarities to the City of Luz. In both accounts the cities are magical; holding keys to spiritual truth, there is only one entrance to the outside world and that is through a secret cave known only to the initiated. The inhabitants essentially live forever and only die when they leave the city. James Hilton, however, was not Jewish and there is no indication that his story was inspired from a Jewish source.

13   Rashi, *Sotah* 46a. Others, however, point out that Rashi's explanation appears to contradict a conclusion elsewhere in the Talmud itself. *Yoma* 54a analyses the scriptural formula "that is its name to this day" where it appears three other times in Tanach. The conclusion is that this phrase does not necessarily imply eternity. However, it is possible to support Rashi's explanation that the phrase "that is its name to this day" implies this by suggesting that the phrase as used here with regard to the second city of Luz is in a different category since it is referring to a actual higher-dimensional reality. In other words, here the simple narrative *pshat* is literally the esoteric secret, i.e., the phrase is literally true but it is referring to another dimen-

sion. In fact, the Talmudic discussion in *Yoma* does not bring our verse from Judges as an example of a case where the elsewhere thrice appearing phrase "that is its name to this day" cannot be understood literally.

14 A question, still to be explored, is who are these peculiar "Hittites", i.e., why do we need to know their name or why not another nationality or foreign land? This is another concealed jewel embedded in the cluster that makes up the secret of the Kingdom of Luz, but this will have to wait for another time.

15 Maharal, *ibid.* concerning as to why it was spiritually necessary that the one who directed the Jewish spies to the secret entrance of Luz had to specifically be from the Canaanite nation. The Maharal's explanation there is also part of unveiling the inner technique of "turning" the key with the polarized Torah Torus, as explained further down in the text.

It is relevant here to draw attention to the most inner nature of the Canaanite. For one familiar with the Torah fractal model this "Luz guide" is a fractal of Metatron. Metatron is variously known, over-simplified, misunderstood and misappropriated as an angel, archangel, demigod, the Lord's servant and "God's right hand man". All these attempted definitions create contradictions and much confusion about the nature of Divine unity. According to orthodox Kabbalah, Metatron is not so much a "person", "place" or "thing" as it is the name and formula for the *entire* system of existence, the instructions on how it runs as well as the instructor himself. Metatron is the Creator's source code for His meta-program that runs *all* the programs of creation. And Metatron the program is also Metatron the programmer. Metatron is called *Sar HaPanim* — Prince of the Face, *Sar Torah* — Prince of Torah, *Sar HaOlam* — Prince of the World and *Ohrpeniel* — Light of the Presence of God. Metatron is the ultimate cosmic chameleon which fractals into an endless array of various micro-*metatrons* and macro-*metatrons*. Metatron is also the guardian of the Luz cave in the mystery of the Canaanite who showed the way. The Talmudic Sage-Mystics' secret of Metatron will be explained at length in a separate book.

16 *Etzem* — literally means both bone and essence. The points along this meridian, from most outward to the most inward, are known by the Talmudic Sage-

Mystics as the luz cave (the occiput), the luz bone (the atlas) and the luz essence (the pineal DMT).

17 There is yet another clue that the Torah has transmitted to us regarding the external and lower nature of the dual aspects of Luz. The Midrash expounds that the word *luz*, although meaning hazelnut, is also related to a verb meaning "to turn aside". In Scripture this word is used mostly in a negative context, either as *"turning away* from wisdom" (Proverbs 3:21, 4:21) or being a *"twisted* person" (Proverbs 3:32, 14:2). The derivative *lazut* means deviation or crookedness and is used only in Proverbs 4:24. The simple explanation as to why the higher-dimensional Luz would also have this connotation is that the Canaanites that lived in the city of Luz (1) before it was conquered by the Israelites were "crooked and perverse". But the perverse nature of the Seven Canaanite tribes that inhabited the land of Canaan is well known throughout the Tanach and thus this meaning of *luz* would not be revealing anything new. Moreover, if the crooked nature of the term *luz* is the sole intention of the sages then why would the Canaanite use the same name for his new and second highly spiritualized city of Luz (2)!? Additionally, this negative connotation of the root meaning of *luz* appears to contradict the pure and highly spiritual nature of the Luz bone discussed below. Rather, it appears that the sages are again revealing the iterating dual nature of luz, i.e., its holy "front side" and its corresponding relatively less holy "backside".

18 This conclusion, also maintained by the Maharal quoted above, appears to be at odds with a fundamental tool of rabbinic and kabbalistic exegesis, "No scriptural verse can be divorced from its literal meaning". This means that, although any given verse unfolds onto many levels of exposition including the homiletic (*drash*), the allegorical or formulaic (*remez*) and the esoteric (*sod*), the plain meaning of the text (*pshat*) must also always be literally true. In our case, a Canaanite man literally did go to the land of the Hittites and built another city that he called Luz. However, the rhetorical question is, "Yes, this is literally true but on what level or *in what dimension* did these events take place"? The ultimate example of this principle is the entire chapter of Adam

and Eve and the serpent. Truly, all rabbis in the orthodox tradition of the Talmudic Sage-Mystics agree on this matter, but both the School of the Gaon of Vilna and the Ramchal are explicit. Everything that Scripture describes as occurring in the Garden of Eden literally occurred but it all occurred in another reality that is extra-dimensional to our current visible existence. This principle, of biblical events literally being true extra-dimensionally, applies throughout the written Torah *when the context demands so*, as is the case here. Simply put by way of analogy, a line is simply a line, but it can also be one quarter segment of a square. An outline of a square can be simply just that — two dimensions (directions) on a planar surface. Concurrently, however, the flat square can also be the single side of a cube — a six-sided three dimensional object. Simultaneously, the cube can still be one side of a tesseract — a hypercube. However, even the hypercube cannot be divorced from its literal "meaning", i.e. it still must conform to and incorporate its 3D, 2D and 1D components. Even in higher-dimensionality a 1D line — the *pshat* is still a 1D line. For more on dimensionality, see my *Beyond Kabbalah*.

19   As known *(Sefer HaBahir* and *Zohar)*, "dead" is an absolutely relative term. Anything that has fallen from it original level is called "dead". Consequently, anything returning to its original level is an aspect of "resurrection". There are, however (as we should expect), different aspects (iterations) of the cosmic principle of *techiyat hamaytim* — resurrection of "dead". They manifest not only collectively (i.e., the general/*klal),* but also individually (i.e., the particular/*prat*). This includes all former *gilgulim* and every age that a person has lived. It also applies in the higher-dimensional future (e.g., the final, global Resurrection of the Dead) as well as in the present (individual Jerusalem of the Mind consciousness).

   Techiyat HaMayteem—the Resurrection or Resuscitation of the Dead—has very little to do with the popular conception of dead bodies emerging from the dust of their graves. Rather, it is an extremely esoteric subject and its higher-dimensional mathematical-like formulations as outlined in advanced Kabbalah are staggering. The underlining principles of this phenomenon go far beyond human bodies, the end of time and reward and punishment. It affects all forms of life, including the animal, plant and mineral kingdoms, the entirety of history and all events in space and time that have ever existed. A full analysis of the profound secret of *Techiyat HaMayteem*, however, requires an essay onto itself. (MP3's of courses and seminars on the subject are available at cityofluz.com)

20 *Otzrot Ramchal Likutim* p. 251. Similarly, the Ramchal's student and colleague writes, "The matter of the Shechinah that remains at the Western Wall and never departs from there is literally the same [i.e., a fractal iteration] as the "vapor of the bones" (R' Moshe David Valli, *Sefer HaLikutim*, p. 355.)

21 It would appear that the breath/vapor emitted from the mouth during prayer and supplications at the Kotel, likely has an iterating correspondence to the vapor of the bones centered in (but not limited to) the Luz/Kotel bone. The almost two thousand years of the prayers by the people of Israel at the Kotel may serve, in effect, as a manifestation on the collective level of the Kotel's living "vapor of the bones". Thus, the millions of prayers that have been "breathed" into the "dead" stones of the Kotel are playing a pivotal role preparing for the future *Techiyat haMayteem*.

22 R' Shmuel HaKatan, *Zikukin d'Nurah u'Biurin d'Aisha*, commentary on *Tanna D'Vei Eliyahu Zuta* Chapter 16.

23 When the luz bone was introduced above I wrote that there is an additional "fourth secret city of Luz". We now understand that it is not so much a city as it is the key hole through which the three cities of Luz are inserted and then "turned" (the unique mode of "toroidal turning" is explained below). Yet, from the source just quoted we see that the luz bone is part of the same hyper-structure, (i.e., in its essence it is also comparable to a "city") and therefore the City(ies) of Luz and the luz(es) of the Spine are one and the same. It is for precisely this reason that the City(ies) and the bone(s) intentionally have the same name — Luz/luz.

24 There are, in fact, two "keyholes", one that is located at the base of the spine and one at the base of the brain. There are two "headquarters", one above and one below. The technology involving the lower "keyhole", and how it interfaces with the upper "keyhole", is more advanced and requires a chapter

onto itself. For our purposes here we will be essentially dealing with the primary headquarters, the luz of the head, but the one who will understand will understand the secret of the lower "keyhole".

25   Notice the Luz iterations connecting the "escorting" of the Shabbat Queen at the time of nurturing the luz bone and the Canaanite escorting the Hebrew warriors to the Luz cave.

26   There are, aside from the names associated with the cities of Luz, some seven terms used by the sages to refer to the complex interface between the human body of this lower dimension and the emergence of the higher-dimensional "new body" and the resurrection of human consciousness. They are (not in a specific order): 1) *etzem haluz* (the luz bone), 2) *luz shel hashidrah* (luz of the spine), 3) *havlay degarmay* (vapor of the bones), 4) *tarvad rakav* (spoonful of [human] decay), 5) *Betuel Rama'ah* (Bethuel the Deceiver), 6) *kusta d'chaiyuta* (spark of life) and 7) *noskoy* ("anointing" or "liquefying substance"). The additional term *tal orot* (dew of lights) is the supernal substance from the higher-dimension that, when "sprinkled" upon the dormant luz essences, will "seed' them from which they will then blossom into eternal life. [A configuration of these seven iterations of Luz and their re-unification can be used to determine the veracity and depth of one's entry into a state of direct experiential Luz consciousness.]

Noskoy is a very unusual term not appearing in Scripture or to be found even in the Talmud, Midrash or Zohar. (Nor in any Hebrew dictionary.) It is a rabbinic neologism of relatively late origin. The earliest reference is found in the *Beit Yosef* commentary on the *Arba'a Turim* where R' Yoseph Karo (The author of the *Shulchan Aruch,* 1488- 1575) writes, "And in the *sidurim* (prayer books) it is explained that there is an *eiver* (limb, appendage, organ) in the human being and its name is *noskoy*. It does not receive pleasure/sustenance from the act of eating except at the departure of the Shabbat *(motza'ai Shabbat)"*. *Noskoy* does not translate into English but its implied meanings are evident. The root of the word is derived from *n-s-ch (nun-samech-chaf)* meaning to pour, to anoint and to consecrate. *"Nesech"* is a libation offering (oil, wine or water) mentioned numerous times in Tanach and in the daily prayer liturgy. It is also the same three letter root meaning "princely" or to make into a prince, i.e., to anoint and elevate to a princely status. Consequently, *noskoy* is alluding to the liquid-like quality of the luz essence as opposed to the rock-like quality of the luz bone. When viewing the Luz hyperstructure we can discern three aspects: the occipital luz "cave", the resurrecting luz "bone" and the liquid luz "essence". All three aspects are necessary for evolving Luz consciousness and entering the Kingdom of Luz. The term *noskoy*, with its analog in the production of molecular DMT, emphasizes the liquid-like nature of the Luz essence. When aroused from its dormant state, its essence is "poured" into the body, anointing and elevating the recipient to a higher princely status.

The Talmudic term, the Aramaic *niskah*, derived from the same root as "to pour", i.e., to pour molten metal, is a gold or silver ingot. Thus, the enigmatic term *noskoy* can also be intentionally alluding to the alchemical-like transformation of a courser substance into a more refined state (as lead into alchemical gold). This would be the parallel process of stimulating the pineal gland to produce and release endogenous DMT, and stimulating the Foundation Stone to produce and release its Living Liquid, as explained in Part I. The fluid state of *noskoy* also interfaces with the phenomenon of the liquidity of the *tal orot*/dew of lights, another aspect of Luz mentioned above.

(*Noskoy*, with its various implicit root meanings, appears to have a number of aspects in common with the discipline of alchemy—the Royal Art—as it was known. Although, with its historical roots in ancient Egypt and Greece, it was during the Middle Ages that the proliferation and practice of alchemy reached a pinnacle and it was during this period that we find the first mention in Torah sources of this specific term. This possible connection is all the more intriguing when we note that virtually all the master alchemists throughout Western history ascribe the origin of this science to the Jews, with the "mother" of all alchemy being the famous Maria Hebraea (the Hebrew or Jewess) from 3rd century C.E. Hellenistic Egypt. Further exploration of the alchemical connection here is needed. See *The Jewish Alchemists — A History and Source Book,* Raphael Patai, 1994, Princeton Press.)

27   *Mishnah Berura,* Laws of Shabbat, chapter 300, #2.

28   *Ibid., Sha'ar HaTzion,* #7 quoting from the Eliyahu Rabba.

29   The Tree of Life and the Tree of Knowledge are, in fact, one "tree", i.e., a higher-dimensional dendrite-like structure. The singularity of the Tree of Life is the trunk and root system of the Tree of Knowledge of Duality (i.e., "good" and "bad") which branches (i.e., scales) outward into lower dimensions. (For more on this subject see *The Secret Doctrine of the Gaon of Vilna,* Volume II, Chapter 2).

30   Another iteration of the same underlying formula is that the First Temple corresponds to the first "upper" *"hey"* of the Tetragrammaton and the Second Temple corresponds to the second "lower" *"hey"* of the Tetragrammaton. (e.g., Arizal, *Eitz Chayim,* Gate 37, Chapter 2). The Third Temple would then correspond to the *"yud"* of the Tetragrammaton (the *"vav"*, which is an extension and "elongation" of the *"yud"*, will then be "drawn back up" into the *"yud"* (along with the upper and lower *"hey"*), as is known in the Kabbalah.

31   This entire continuum, as known in the Kabbalah, is a spectrum of *da'at* and *yesod* — the two being fundamentally one and the same. When the *da'at* energy is at the base of the spine it is identified as *yesod* and when *yesod* energy is at the top of the spine it is identifies as *da'at*. In turn, when the same *yesod/da'at* energy is in the middle of the brain, i.e., the place of the pineal, it is identified as the upper *da'at* to distinguish it from the lower *da'at* at the base of the head. The upper *da'at* is also the bridge uniting the two lobes of the brain — the right and left hemispheres. As such, the term (upper) *da'at* can also correspond to the corpus callosum and, by extension, to other midbrain structures.

32   Tractate *Sotah* 46b.

33   As known, in a *machloket*/dispute regarding a *halachic*/legal conflict, the matter must be adjudicated and one view will be designated the primary law and accepted practice while the "rejected" view (or views) remains the minority view. However, in matters of Aggadah — the Talmudic genre of non-legal discussions (which make up a quarter to one-third of the entire Talmud!) —

one view is never more "binding" than another, as none of the views affect any legal or ritual decision. Moreover, as stated, "These and those are both the words of the Living God", i.e., that all of the rabbinic views in an aggadic discussion ultimately must be true simultaneously and the full picture will not emerge until all the components are assembled and superimposed one upon the other.

34 In order to gain a glimpse of how this inter-dimensional brotherhood communicated one with another we can use the mathematical/computer model of an algorithm: a set of rules that precisely define a sequence of operations for solving a problem (In computereze this is known as a "macro"). The Talmudic Sage-Mystics, throughout their aggadic formulations, are generating hundreds—even thousands—of esoteric algorithms. Accordingly, all the components of their "conversations" must be used because they were all *intended* to be used—even the elements of the Aggadic episodes and the sages' own statements that they seem to be rejecting! Virtually every single word of these masters is sequencing hidden Torah algorithms.

Consequently, Talmudic Aggadah is as much about the practice and study of revealing information as it is about the practice and study of hiding information. Aggadah and Midrash is nothing less than rabbinic cryptography. The aggadic passages, be they one-line maxims or pages and pages of mythical sounding "stories", are a unique form of kabbalistic *encryption*. Encryption is the process of converting ordinary information ("plaintext") into unintelligible gibberish (the "cipher text"). In the case with the Talmudic Sage-Mystics, they are converting unimaginable kabbalistic secrets—here the plain text being the *pshat*/narrative of the *sod*/secret—into virtually unintelligible gibberish—the cipher text of the ostensibly outlandish and impossible tales and "legends" of the Talmud!

A sub-category of cryptography is steganography and it is an even more accurate model of what the sages are doing. Steganography is hiding a secret message within a larger one in such a way that others cannot discern the presence or contents of the hidden message. It is the art and science of writing hidden messages such that no one, apart from the sender and intended recipient, suspects the existence of the message—no one even knows there is a secret message that has been encoded! It is a form of "security through obscurity". Whereas the standard cryptographic encryption protects the contents of a message from "outsiders", steganography protects both the messages and the communicating parties—in our case, the Talmudic masters. Though the medium of Aggadah only the sages know who they are transmitting to and who understands what they are transmitting. The "outsiders" and "external elements" don't even know that a form of "meta-communication" among the Talmudic Sage-Mystics, spanning millennia and all around the globe, is occurring.

35   The relationship of the "one mouth" and "two fingers" can also iterate as a cylindrical tube with its two openings protruding its two fingers into itself from both directions simultaneously, i.e., the two funnels forming a donut-like form. Instead of the formulation of a "mouth-finger-finger", this would be formulated as a "finger-mouth-finger". This is the very Torah Torus structure itself explained below.

36   The word torus comes from a Latin word meaning cushion, i.e., the geometrical toroidal form resembles a Roman cushion. (It is intriguing to note that at the site of *Beit El*/Luz Jacob used the Foundation Stone as a pillow or cushion that he placed under the back of his head (and/or "around his head") at the place of his luz cave/bone/essence. Accordingly, the torus has again brought us back full circle to the intrinsic connection between toroidal space and the secret of Luz.)

37   Brian Greene, *The Elegant Universe*, 1999 N.Y.

38   Itzak Bentov, *Stalking the Wild Pendulum* and *A Brief Tour of Higher Consciousness*.

39   Author Gary Osborn, Internet, http://garyosborn.webs.com/ dimensiondoorways.htm.

40   The Gaon's commentary to the Zohar's *Sifra diTzniuta*, Chapter 1, "Graving of engravings like the appearance of an elongated serpent..." and the *Leshem's* commentary to the Gra in *Hakdamot u'Sh'arim, Likutim*, from p. 192 to p. 201 with the *Leshem's* graphic on p. 197. The *Leshem* elsewhere explains (*Sefer Dayah*, Part II, p. 179):

The Holy [macro] Serpent is the fountainhead, root and essence for all of God's sacred, revelatory Light, from which emanate all dimensions of reality. This is the ray of Light of the Ain Sof that extends into the *tzimtzum*. This ray of light is what becomes the "supernal pathways of the image of the elongating [macro] Serpent, which stretches out on both sides with its tail [united] in its head, its head "returning upon its shoulders". This [serpent] is the secret of the Cosmic Balance, the Supernal *Da'at* (the middle brain of the Godhead). This is Leviathan, [which splits into its two aspects of] the straight serpent and the curved serpent. Its root is from the penetrating and surrounding Light of the *Ain Sof*. The aspect of the straight serpent that stands in the "middle" is the letter *vav* in the word *gachon* (belly), which is in the middle of all the letters of the Torah. And because it is the central axis that extends from end to end [of reality], therefore the *vav* of "belly" is an elongated macro-*vav*. Now, from this Supernal *Da'at* emanates the entirety of the Torah. From here also is the source of Moses' soul. Therefore Moses is also called by the appellation of Leviathan, the "straight" serpent, as it is written in the Zohar. And it is this Supernal *Da'at* that is the source of the Concealed Light through which one can see from one end of the universe to the other. It is this radiance that [emanates as] the secrets of the Torah. Moses our Teacher, who emanates from the macro-vav of the "belly" — Leviathan the straight serpent, the Supernal *Da'at* — drew upon this Concealed Light throughout his entire life.

41 The Zohar's term for the area where the straight serpent reunites with its own self is *kudlah* (as also written in the original diagram) which is the Aramaic term for the back or nape of the neck. This is the area of the occiput, the vortex of the *da'at*, the "middle brain". This term, and especially in its plural form *kudlay* and *kudalin*, is uncannily similar to the ancient Sanskrit term "kundalini" and the entire Oriental tradition of Kundalini yoga and associated tantric practice. The significance of this spiritual "coincidence" is subject for another chapter although the framework is laid out in my essay *The Return of the Children of the East*.

Simply put, this Leviathanic circuit can be worn as an internal "wreath" encircling the cranium. This is done by visually entering from the occiput at an incline creating an axis running from just below the occipital ridge through the pineal gland. The circuit then exits at the hairline which then splits into right and left "tails" returning to the "head" of the serpent. Likewise, this entire process is visually and experientially replicated by entering through the "lower *kudlah*", i.e., the lower luz vortex at the perineum, with the "two tails" splitting at the upper *kudlah,* i.e., the upper luz vortex, and returning to the serpent head embedded in the perineum and its iterations. The secret of the Two-Tailed Leviathan is also the template to the full story of the male and female Leviathan and the future, i.e., higher-dimensional Feast of Leviathan.

42 The two-tailed Leviathanic dynamic also iterates in the secret of the Twin Messiahs. (For more on Leviathan see Chapter 3 of *The Secret Doctrine of the Gaon of Vilna* and Chapter 1 there for more on the Twin Messiahs.

43 Ironically, this symbol is more "Jewish" than the now universally recognized six-pointed "Star of David", whose worldwide recognized symbology is only several centuries old. Even the symbol of the seven branched menorah used in the *Mishkan*/Tabernacle and in the two Temples is not as archetypal and core to Torah consciousness as is this virtually unknown esoteric Jewish Uroboros.

44 See my *Beyond Kabbalah — the Teachings That Cannot Be Taught,* Door of Models.

45 This is also known as the dance of the *Hasadim* and *Gevurot* — the Creator's straight, expanding, masculine light and curved, contracting, feminine light. This is the polarity from which you produce the fuel for the stimulation to go into Luz. The goal is to always maintain tension between your positive and negative terminals wherever you are, be it in your upper luz or your lower luz, your physical body or your soul body, your micro-form or your macro-form. It is this somatic-psychic, electromagnetic energy that you generate that keeps your spiritual gyroscope spinning. One becomes, in effect, an organic battery generating the feminine *gevurot* that stimulate the masculine *hasadim* to radiate back down to feed the *gevurot* to stimulate the *hasadim,* etc., each pole looped into the other. It is this arc of constant polarity that supplies the current or the "spiritual electricity" to run and animate the Torah Torus.

46 There are an ever growing array of unusual and very bizarre looking tori that have been emerging from the fields of higher-dimensional mathematics, surface topology and string theory (M-Theory), as well as also from creative graphic artists pushing the limits of geometry and CGI.

47 The term used in the verse is *mevoh ha-ir*, meaning entrance. However, it more literally translates as [point of] intercourse or transaction. The root of *mevoh* is the same as *biah*/conjugal union. It implies an exchange of a dynamic process that is taking place. Again we see that the aspect of the physical must be used here in order to enter the spiritual. See above end of note 4.

48 The relationship between a bell and its clapper also has esoteric significance. The hem of the robe worn by the Kohen Gadol is adorned with seventy two golden bells each with its own clapper. Additionally, on the hem were seventy two "pomegranates" woven from colored wool. Pomegranates, as known from the Arizal, are in the secret of Metatron and the clapper and bell are iterating aspects of *Zeir Anpin* and his *Nukbah*.

49 Aryeh Kaplan, *Inner Space*, Maznaim Publishing Corporation, N.Y. and Israel, p. 3, note 12 and p. 32, drawing upon both classical Torah and kabbalistic sources.

50 "Therefore see that the first letters of the three words, ""From between the two *keruvim*" are *m-sh-hey* spelling Moshe. This is because his prophecy [and consequently all prophecy, as Moses is the root-source of all the prophets, as is known] was drawn from that source". R' Moshe David Valle, loc. cit.

51 This was not solely a Hollywood invention. The Ark did indeed have unique innate powers. Notably is the case when the Philistines captured the Ark from the Jews. Wherever it was taken the Philistines were stricken with sickness and plague. This continued for seven months until they returned the Ark to the Jews (I Samuel chs. 4-6). There is also the case of the grave miscalculation of the two sons of Aaron, Nadav and Avihu. The Torah records that, upon offering "alien fire" that was not prescribed at that time, and "A fire came forth from before HaShem and consumed them" (Leviticus 10:2). The fire came forth from the Holy of Holies. Presumably the fire came from the Ark of the Covenant. Additionally we are taught, "When Israel were on their journeys, two sparks of fire would emerge from the two staves to [carry] the Ark to strike down their enemies" (Midrash Rabbah, Numbers 5:1).

52   There is almost no prohibition in the Torah that, under specific conditions and at one time or another, overrides its own general law. There are "human based", i.e., rational or philosophical reasons explaining these anomalies, but the deeper truth behind these exceptions requires knowledge of advanced Kabbalah. In the case of the *keruvim*, however, a partial explanation is this: the prohibition of constructing 3D figures only applies in our 3D "Flatland" reality. In a higher-dimensional reality there is no corresponding prohibition because that realm is spatially non-local as well as non-temporal! But this explanation should never apply in our lower reality as there is no place here that is not 3D Flatland! However, there is an exception — the Holy of Holies. This space, while its external spatial coordinates are anchored in "this world", it also co-exists in a higher-dimension. The *Kadosh Kodoshim* is a Jewish "star-gate", the "Gate to Heaven" and the *Makom*-Place of the world. The prohibition of making or having idols does not apply there because within the "space" of the Holy of Holies the *keruvim* also literally exist in a higher-dimension where the prohibition does not apply.

The fact that the *keruvim* existed in a multi-dimensional reality is an accepted tradition by the Talmud. Architecturally, according to the precise measurements of the Holy of Holies, there could not have been enough room for the wingspan of the two *keruvim*. "The space taken up by the Ark and the *keruvim* is not included in the dimensions of the Holy of Holies". (Tractate *Bava Batra* 99a). Additionally, it is a Talmudic tradition that the two *keruvim*, under specific conditions "came alive" and moved on their own. Thus, when Israel was fulfilling the will of the Omnipresent (lit., the "*Makom*"!) they would face each other. If the opposite was true then they would turn askance from each other (*Ibid.* 99a).

53   Talmud *Avodah Zarah*, 3b.

54   Rashi, 3:24 quoting the Midrash.

55   Radak, Chizkuni, loc. cit.

56   R' Meyuchas (The name of the sage is not known), brought in ArtScroll Bereishis.

57   Midrash Rabbah, 21:9.

58   R' Shimshon Raphael Hirsch, 1808-1888.

59 *Inner Space,* p. 177.

60 *Ibid.* p. 230, note 242.

61 For those P2P practitioners who have experienced the methodology of the Luz cruise, this verse is referring to what may be the ultimate *Luz Keruv Cruise!*

62 A more advanced practitioner may want to know that the polarized set of the *keruvim* of the Ark are situated at the opening of the "lower" Gan Eden, i.e., at the base of the Adamic spine (Also iterating as the lower Luz cave and luz bone at the base of the spine). The polarized set of the *keruvim* of Gan Eden are situated at the "higher" Gan Eden, i.e., the top of the spine of the Adamic structure (Also iterating as the upper Luz cave and luz bone at the top of the spine).

63 Other sources indicate that the *Sefer Torah* was lying on the outside of the Ark and that a cruse of the anointing oil, container of the manna and the staff of Aaron with its almonds and blossoms were also inside with the Ten Commandments (Tractate *Yoma* 52b). We can assume that wherever the Ark was stationed it was also zooming into and amplifying that specific coordinate of space where it was resting. This is logical due to the holographic and fractal nature of reality that requires there to be a little bit of Jerusalem everywhere in the world and thus a potential microcosmic portal back to the original, higher-dimensional Garden of Eden.

Fundamentally, with practice the golden *keruvim* alone can align with one's pineal gland and open up the inner temple vortex. This is the essence of the P2P *Keruvim* HeadSet. However, on a more advanced level, and certainly if one wants to accelerate the process, the secret will be in training oneself to superimpose the set of Gan Eden *keruvim* onto the Ark *keruvim* and vice versa. Now, if we only knew what those Gan Eden *keruvim* look like! Almost by definition it would seem that this is impossible as how can one focus on, "the flame of the ever-turning sword". The Midrash quoted above informs us that "Sometimes they appear as men, sometimes as women, sometimes as spirits, sometimes as angles". This appears as a frenetic, chaotic hallucination that has no single image at all!

However, if we understand the "sword" here as a "blade" then the opposite is true. Imagine an airplane propeller where one blade is the body of a "man" and its corresponding opposite blade is the body of a "woman" and another blade is the essence of a "spirit" and its corresponding opposite blade is the essence of an "angel". Now, when that propeller blade is turned on and animated, what do you see? If one knows how to "see" with slightly higher dimensional consciousness, then the composite image (a coherent superposition) of what one will behold is a conscious membrane of, for lack of any more suitable terms, "divine skin". It is this higher-dimensional "flesh" that is the outer "texture" and "form" of the Gan Eden *keruvim*. One does not need to know (and cannot know) the actual shape or appearance of these *keruvim*. Rather, all we need is their "skin" and then, like ever-changing "computer skins", superimpose it upon the golden *keruvim*. This is the secret of the two sets of *keruvim* that are, fundamentally, one in the same

64 Talmud *Succah* 5b.

65 Talmud *Yoma* 54a.

66 For more explanation of the "small" *keruvim* vs. the "large" *keruvim* see R' Moshe David Valle (disciple and colleague of Ramchal) in his commentary to Genesis 3:24. The Arizal writes explicitly that the *keruvim* on the Ark simultaneously were iterations of the *partzufim* of *Abba* and *Imma* (the adult aspect) and *Zeir Anpin* and his *Nukbah* (the younger aspect) as well as the two sefirot of *Nezach* and *Hod*. Moreover, different modes of *keruvim* exist within each of the four dimensions/worlds. *Sefer HaLikutim Terumah*. See also *Kehilot Yaakov*, s.v. *keruvim*.

67 This phenomenon is also prophesied in the verse, "All the nations of the world will see that the Name of HaShem is called upon you, and they will be in awe of you" (Deut. 28:10). According to the Sages the "Name of HaShem" here refers to the tefillin of the head which has within it the name *Shadai* which equals 214 which equals Metatron and all of their iterations. Metatron is *Sar HaPanim*, Lord of the Face/Innerface/Interface which is Peniel – the Face of God. (See Talmud Bavli *Berachot* 6a and Talmud Yerushalmi *Berachot* 54b).

68 Joel 3:1.

69 A full page color copy of the P2P Keruvim HeadSet is available at no cost. Just email me: jbakst@cityofluz.com

70 The number 49 is only being used because it is segues into a more advanced level of P2P. The Hebrew letters *mem* and *tet* equal 49, a primary value associated with Metatron and which is also abbreviated with the two letters *mem* and *tet*. Regarding Metatron see note 16 to Part II Chapter 1.

71 Once again, you have to be true to yourself. You may experience yourself slowly "floating" up the stairs or through the tunnel. You simply want what works the quickest and best for you.

72 DMT professional Terrence McKenna quoted above in Part I.

73 *Epistle to Yemen*, based upon the verse from the Book of Joel quoted above.

74 See the endnote to Part I Chapter 5, The River of Light: Global DMT.

75 Talmud *Pesachim* 112a.

The Author

Joel David Bakst is a teaching rabbi and scholar of Talmud, Kabbalah and Biblical Hebrew who, for 20 years while living in Jerusalem, studied and taught in Orthodox yeshivot. He has lectured and given workshops in Israel, the United States and India. He has written extensively about the confluence of Kabbalah and science with a special interest in the biblical and kabbalistic references to the pineal gland and the DMT model as it relates to higher consciousness and global evolution. He lives and teaches in Southern Colorado.

His published books are the two companion volumes, *The Secret Doctrine of the Gaon of Vilna: The Messianic Role of Torah, Kabbalah and Science* and *The Josephic Messiah, Leviathan, Metatron and the Sacred Serpent. Beyond Kabbalah: The Teachings That Cannot Be Taught* will soon be available. His books, recordings and classes are available at cityofluz.com.

Made in the USA
San Bernardino, CA
28 November 2014